ZELMA
HIGH'MONEY

LET
GOD
BE TRUE AND
LIVE

THE GOSPEL OF
JESUS CHRIST

WESTBOW
PRESS
A DIVISION OF THOMAS NELSON

WestBow Press books may be ordered through booksellers or by contacting:

WestBow Press
A Division of Thomas Nelson
1663 Liberty Drive
Bloomington, IN 47403
www.westbowpress.com
1-(866) 928-1240

ISBN: 978-1-4497-6020-5 (sc)
ISBN: 978-1-4497-6740-2 (e)
Library of Congress Control Number: 2012912863

Printed in the United States of America

WestBow Press rev. date: 4/16/2013

WORDS ABOUT THE AUTHOR

God told me in 1980 to write a book. By me not knowing that was God talking to me, I responded by saying "oh no, not me!, I don't know a thing about writing a book' That was on Thursday and on Saturday my mom called me and we talked maybe about 20 minutes and hung up the phone and mom called me right back and said Zelma, God said for you to write a book. I responded by saying, "ooh that was God who was talking to me? By not understanding that was God speaking to me, He told my mom what he wanted me to do. God has given me a witness every step of the way concerning this book and my ministry and concerning the church. Mom and Dad always kept their children in church and I never left the church until God made me come out. I was the fourth child of eleven children. Dad said as I was being born, the Holy Spirit said to him, "this child is chosen", my dad preached that over the pulpit as long as he lived. God revealed my calling to me concerning the work I was chosen to do in 1991. About five years after a minister whom I had never seen, prophesied to me and told me that God was bringing me into an unusual ministry.

This prophetic message came to me about 1986. Five years before I received my calling from the Lord. The second prophetic message came in 1990. About one year before I received my calling from the Lord, both prophetic messages was the same, that God was bringing me into an unusual ministry and these two prophets did not know each other.. These messages was prophesied to me about the period of four years of each other and about three years later in 1993, God sent a messenger to me whom I had never seen, by the name of Karl Stokes with the message and the knowledge of eternal life without having to die. It was the strangest thing I had ever heard. I was taught that you had to die before you get eternal life. I never heard this scripture taught before, If a man keep my sayings he shall never die (John 8:51). I had heard ministers preach the gospel of Peter and of Paul but I have never heard anybody preach the message about Jesus sayings. I was totally blind to what Jesus sayings meant.

DEDICATION OF BOOK

I want to dedicated this book to my precious deceased mother and father Holbert and Corene Holmes, who loved their children and loved God with all their heart and with all their understanding, and to my four sisters, Alma Freeman, Edna Bishop, Ruby Brown and Frances Anthony, whom I hope will not allow fear and unbelief to hinder them from reading this book; to the memory of my deceased sisters; Reable Byrd and, Ethel Hall, to my four brothers; Holbert Holmes Jr, and Kenneth Ray Holmes, to the memories of my deceased brothers; Harold Holmes and Joe Holmes: to my nine children; Travis Jeter, Clarence Jeter, Deborah Jeter Bonman, Irben Jeter, LaTonia Johnson Davis, Karla Johnson Tyson, Holbert Johnson, William Johnson, to my god daughter, Bisi Waddell and to the memory of my deceased son Jan Jerome Johnson: and to their spouses and friends, past and present; Sandra, June, Elise, Emlyne, Andrea, Crystal, Deborah Sweet, LaTonya, Ben. Jason, Lisa Darden, Christine Meland, Sandra, Catherine, Lee Davis II, Charles Bonman, Willie Tyson, Denise, Delphine, Alexes, Charles Robinson, Michael, Thuy, Song, Susie, Angelo, Steven:

To my thirty two grandchildren; Travis Jr, Tessa, Aisha, Monique, Charles Jr, Alvin, Danny Jr, Darryl, Tonisha, Irben Jr, Tomiko, Lee Jr, Lamont, Derrick, Vernisha, Daniel, Clarence, Jeffery, Tori. Holbert Jr, Brandon, Jessika, Nathan, Jonathan, Joshua, Christopher, Garrett, Melanie, Spechel, Preston, Madison, Xavier, to my twenty some odd great grandchildren; Elijah, Isaiah, Ashley, Krystile, Brittiney, Erica, Myriah the competitive cheer leader: Keith, Khalil, Tylen, Kaitlin, Leanna, Lee Davis IV, Darius, Jesse, Kaylani, Joel, Jasmine, Darious, Donald, Tyshun, Destiny, Daniel, Jounie, Heaven. Jeremy, Sky, Sean, to my one great, great granddaughter, Aaliyah, who is my fifth generation; and to all my nieces and nephews: to: my nephews, Harold Holmes Jr and Marco Riley. I dedicate my book to a lovely family, Jackie and Dave Reese, Jasmine and Martha; to my sister in Christ, Arona Sanford; to my good friend Essie Davis, to my dear friend, Evang, Mary Jones; to my amazing friend Esmeraldo Quintera; to my playmate, Velma Hayes; also I dedicate my book to my friend, Sister Irene Shumate, and to Dorothea, a young woman who confesses that she love Jesus, who is by faith, Jehovah Witness; and to Mother Liz Wilson and also to those who listened to me in agreement and said to me that they understand what I was talking about; and to every Church who believe in Jesus: I pray that God through his mercy will grant each of you; that the eyes of your understanding be enlightened that you may know what the hope of his calling is, may the grace and mercy of God rest upon each of you who read this book. Amen.

ACKNOWLEDGEMENT

I acknowledge a Spirit filled man of God, Dr. Harlo White who have been such an encouragement to me through his ministry by CD's and Audio Tapes and his indescribable teaching of the mysteries of God on eternal life, God told me in 1997 to plant seeds in the Harlo White Ministries and I have continued to plant that seed to support that great ministry, I also acknowledge my former pastor, Bishop BR. Benbow who taught me the principals of faith in the word of God. I want to acknowledge my eleven year old granddaughter, Spechel Jeter who so beautifully wrote an outstanding tribute for my book and wanted to share it by adding it to my acknowledgements. It was so moving to my spirit and I am so grateful for her. I pray that it will also bless others who read it. Spechel writes; "When you try to find a path, find God's path because he cares for you the way we care for him" Thank you Spechel. I acknowledge Attorney Joseph R. Evann of Los Angeles, who will never know how much he encouraged me concerning my faith, I acknowledge Brother Karl Stokes, the messenger that God sent to me with the Kingdom message of eternal life.

LET GOD BE TRUE AND LIVE THE GOSPEL OF JESUS CHRIST

This book is written and totally based on scripture and the gospel of Jesus Christ. God has given me the knowledge and the revelations of the gospel of Jesus Christ to equip me to write these scriptural truths. That the eyes of your understanding being enlightened; that you may know what the hope of his calling is for you. (Eph.1:18-22). All scripture is given by the inspiration of God (2 Tim.3-16). Jesus himself said the scripture could not be broken; (John 10:35). Whose gospel's you going to believe the gospel of Jesus and live or the gospel of man and die? The gospel of Jesus Christ should be considered the highest authority of all the gospels by everyone. Jesus said in (St. John 8:51) "Verily, verily, I say unto you, if a man keep (my sayings) he shall never see death. The sayings of Jesus are the prophecies of Jesus that the angel of the Lord was testifying about in the book of Revelation. For I testify unto every man that heareth the words of the prophecy of this book, if any man shall add unto these things, God shall add unto him the plagues that are written in this book. The plagues are sickness, disease and death. And if any man shall take away from the words of the book of this prophecy, God shall take away his part out of the book of life, (Rev.22:18,19). Which mean you will not have eternal life. Keeping Jesus sayings, is saying what he say. His sayings are his prophecies and his prophecies are his gospel. In the olden days prophecies were called sayings even when I was a child; although some would call them say-on. Jesus said if you keep my sayings you will never die, man say "repent and get saved so you'll be ready to die" get ready to die is not Jesus sayings that is man's saying, Jesus said if any man hear these sayings of mine and do them, he will be liken unto a wise man; (Matt.7:21-29). Jesus said except you repent ye shall likewise perish: (Luke 13:5). So whose gospel are you going to obey? Are you going to repent and live as Jesus said, or repent to prepare to die as man said? The choice is yours. God said I set before you this day, life and good,-death and evil, he said therefore choose life, (Deut.30:15, 19). You have the choice to live or die, live is the way God planned it. God wouldn't have said choose life if he didn't mean it. God don't play games. He said, God is not a man that he should lie (Numbers 23:19). I am not preaching Fire and Brimstone I'm preaching life, neither am I condemning anybody. You are the captain of your own soul and everybody has to give an account of the deeds that is done in their body.

THE DOCTRINE OF DEATH

Death is a doctrine that has been adopted into the churches by men. Before Adam sinned it was not God's will for death to reign in our mortal bodies, that's why Jesus died. He came to redeem his people back from sin and death. Sin brought about death. Let not sin reign or dwell in your mortal body: (Romans 6:12). That as sin hath reigned unto death, even so might grace reign through righteousness, (which is faith) unto eternal life by Jesus Christ our Lord. (Rom.5:21): For God so loved the world that he give his only begotten son that who so even believeth in him <u>should</u> <u>not</u> <u>die</u>; (John 3:16). Notice that scripture did not say: who so even believeth in him shall not perish, but it said they should not perish, if they should not perish, why are they perishing? There is something not right about that: the churches of God need to check that out.

When the first Adam sinned and brought about sin and death on himself and everybody else, at that moment God began to search for a way to bring his people from under that sinful and death nature that Adam brought on the churches of God. Therefore God chose Abraham and called him his friend. Abraham was a man full of faith (full of righteousness) and was obedient to God. God counted Abraham's faith as righteousness, (James 2:21-23). God sent an angel to tell Abraham he was going to bless him with a son. When his wife Sarah heard that she laughed because she and Abraham were up in age and had past the age of child bearing. The angel ask Sarah why did she laugh, she replied, oh I didn't laugh. She did not have the faith that Abraham had. Consequently she gave Abraham her hand maid to sleep with so she could bare him a son and after the child was born Sarah became jealous and told Abraham to cast out the bond woman and her son. God told Abraham to harken unto his wife voice by casting out his son and the bond's woman. God told Abraham that he was going to make his son by the bond woman a nation. Abraham obeyed and at one hundred years old, God blessed him with the son of promise whose name was Isaac. God tested Abraham two times, first by telling him to harken unto his wife voice and cast out his son by the bond woman and Abraham obeyed; the second time God told him to offer up his son Isaac for a sacrifice and again Abraham obeyed God; look at it, when you think about Abraham's life concerning his sons, it were on the same order as God, concerning his son, by obedient Abraham cast out his first born son and the bond's woman, so did God cast out Adam out of the garden of Eden. By obedient to God, Abraham offered his second son Isaac for a sacrifice who was his son of promise. God offered his son Jesus who was the son of promise for the sacrifice for our sins. Jesus paid the price to redeem us from the death that Adam brought on us, so we won't have to die. What a mighty God we have. Jesus was the Sacrificing Lamb who was slain for the redemption of those who believe. (Rev.5:12). God saw Abraham's obedience and told him, now Abraham I know that you love me and because of your obedient I am going to make you the father of many nations. God chose the linage of Abraham that he might go down and save his people from their sin. God came down through forty two generations: all the generations from Abraham to David are fourteen generations and from David to the carrying away into Babylon are fourteen generations and from the carrying away into Babylon unto Christ are fourteen generations. There God chose a woman whose name was Mary, a woman whom God could count worthy to bring forth his Son Jesus, who was born in Bethlehem, who went about doing good, preaching the good news of eternal life, healing the sick, raising the dead and died by hanging on a tree for our sins and rising again on the third day and declared he was alive for ever more. Jesus said because I live you shall live also. (St. John 14:19). The believers were set free from sin and death, until death was revived in the churches by the teaching and preaching of men indoctrinating the church to prepare to die: by telling them when they die they will go to heaven, God never intended for those who believed in his Son to die.

Before Paul came to know Jesus as his personal savior he was one who went about persecuting the churches, because the apostles was preaching and teaching this same message. Paul didn't believe that Jesus Christ was the son of God and that Jesus was the messiah who came to save his people (the church) from sin. The people were looking for a king to come but not the kind who could <u>save</u> people from (<u>dying</u>). Paul who was called Saul was breathing out threats against the church and the disciples of the Lord. He went to the high priest and desired of him letters to Damascus to the Synagogues that if he found any in that way of preaching Jesus, that he might bring them bound unto Jerusalem. As he came near Damascus; suddenly there shined round about him a light from heaven, he fell to the earth and heard a voice saying unto him, Saul, Saul, why persecute thou me and Saul answered, who are thy Lord? The Lord said I am Jesus whom thou persecute. Jesus told Saul everything that would befall him because of the preaching of the gospel that he was ordaining him to preach. Jesus gave Paul, who was called Saul instructions of what to do. Saul was without sight for three days. The Lord showed him in a vision that there will be one named Ananias whom God had instructed to lay hands on him that he might receive his sight. Saul obeyed and went to Damascus and received his sight. Then was Saul certain days with the disciples which was at Damascus and straightway he went to the synagogues and began preaching the gospel of Jesus Christ and remained there for three years. Afterward he met with the disciples and did the greater work of them all. (Acts 9:1-22).

The Apostle Paul said for I am not ashamed of the gospel of Christ, for it is the power of God unto salvation to everyone that believeth. (Rom.1:16). There were many in that day who didn't want to hear the gospel of Jesus Christ preached, the same as it is today. They don't want to hear the full complete gospel of Jesus Christ preached because of their unbelief and preaching of the doctrine of death. Before Jesus came the people had no knowledge of eternal life. Eternal life was the good news that Jesus came preaching. Before that, all the people knew or ever heard of was death and dying and getting ready to die. Which is caused by the sin of unbelief and for the lack of knowledge that Jesus died that we might live, even today they don't understand his gospel because the complete and full gospel is not preached in the churches. Jesus said repent you therefore that you might live. In the churches they preach repent so you will be ready to die. The Apostles knew that the Gospel of Jesus Christ was a strange and unusual gospel. While some were still dying because of unbelief which is sin; they continued to preach the gospel of Jesus Christ to as many who would receive it. Jesus had commissioned the disciples and apostles to preach the gospel and declare that he had abolished death and had brought life and immortality to light though the gospel. (2 Tim.1:10). Those who believed in his gospel and keep his sayings would have eternal life; here they were preaching and telling people that Jesus died to redeem them from the curse of sin and death, and had taken away death by hanging on a tree and rising again on the third day.

Many Christian continued to die because of unbelief and for the lack of knowledge, Jesus said because I live you shall live also, (St. John 14:19) Jesus said behold I am alive for evermore. (Rev 1:18).

The apostles continued to preach the gospel of Jesus Christ which is eternal life. There was a great controversy because of that gospel. The people were afraid of change, just as they are today, although change meant to live and not die. People were skeptical about accepting the change that Jesus preached about and they are still skeptical. The apostles continued to preach and spread the good news and the anointing was great and the supernatural power of God was powerful, because they had the fear of God, the people were careful how they came into the presence of God; Ananias and Sap-phi-r-a was a great example of what could happen. They could not stand in the presence of God and of the Holy Ghost and lie. When they lied they both fell dead (Acts.5:1-5). That brought about a greater fear on the church. The churches were powerful because of the fear of God and the preaching of the gospel of Jesus Christ. Even when I was a young woman because of that scripture of what happened to Ananias and Sap-phi-r-a the church still had the fear of God. Which caused it to have more power than it have today, especially the churches that was called Spirit filled churches or the Pentecostal churches. The scripture said the fear of God is the beginning of wisdom(Prov.9:10):. You could hardly pay a person to come into the church in the presence of God and in the mist of the saints and start some kind of brawl lest knowing shooting and killing people in the churches as they are doing today or some other bad things that they do; they would be slain under the anointing and the power of the Holy Ghost and when they would come to themselves or get up off the floor, they were a different person. Sometimes the Holy Spirit would reveal and bring somebody to an open shame if they were confessing to be saved and were doing some ungodly thing. It would sometimes be revealed by the Holy Ghost: a family member went to a church a few Sundays ago and there was middle aged Bishop there who said "I am so tired of these preachers preaching death" I said oh my God there is a man according to God's own heart. God said: I will give you pastors according to mine heart, (which shall feed you with knowledge and understanding) (Jeremiah 3:15) the underlined part is what you never hear a preacher preach or talk about, you would think that scripture ended with, I give you pastors according to mine heart: God didn't say I will give you pastors which shall feed you with death, by telling you to prepare yourself to die so you'll go to heaven. He said, I will give you pastors which: shall feed you with knowledge; the knowledge that pastors get by seeking to know God; and the knowledge that God said that you perish for the lack of. You don't know him just by getting saved and filled with the Holy Ghost or even when you are called to preach, that's just the beginning. You have to seek to know God. All through the bible God say seek to know me.

There were two special circumstances where God spoke about death, He said. Precious in the sight of the Lord is the death of his saints. (Psalms 116:15). He was not saying, Precious is the death that his saints died, he were saying precious is the death of his saints who was killed for his sake and the sake of the gospel. God said I have no pleasure in the death of him that die, there-fore turn yourselves and live; said the Lord. (Ezek.18:32) God said be ye faith unto death and I will give you a crown of life, (Rev.2:10) <u>he didn't say be faithful until you die,</u> he said be faithful unto death, he's talking about when your adversary threaten to kill you for preaching the gospel of God and of Jesus Christ, don't stop preaching his gospel because somebody threatening to kill you, be faithful, continue to preach as the apostles, John, Steven, Peter and Paul and many others did. Whose death was because of the preaching of the gospel of Jesus Christ, they were the ones who were faithful unto death, they didn't die what you call a natural death they were killed because they continued to be faithful by preaching the gospel of Christ. You don't have to be doing anything bad or disobey any commandments to commit a sin and die, all you have to do is not believe or not keep Jesus sayings, that's all it take and you have sinned and because of sin you die. The reason the gospel of Jesus Christ has remained to be strange and unusual to the churches is because the preachers are not preaching it, when you begin preaching the full gospel it will no longer be strange and neither would it be strange to hear a person say I know I will never die or I shall be changed from this mortal to immortality.

The messenger that God sent to me by the name of Karl Stokes: called me every day which seemed for about three months, preaching the message of eternal life to me, for the lack of knowledge I called it stuff and mess. One day I felt so fed up with him and what I called his mess, I said to myself I can't listen to this mess anymore. I said who does he think I am to be listening to this stuff; I said when he call me this evening I'm going to tell him don't call me anymore and I mean don't call me anymore. That evening he called as usual, and I said to him, that scripture that you always quote to me. I was trying not to seem as unsaved as I though he was, so I started off talking about a scripture. But as many as receive him to them he gave the power to become the sons of God, even to them that believe on his name, (St. John 1:12) I said to him; "I kind of understand that scripture, although my church don't dwell on it, but the rest of that stuff you are talking about, forget it! my next words was going to be, don't call me anymore and I mean don't call me anymore, instantly I heard the Holy Spirit say, "if you can understand that scripture, why don't you ask God to reveal to you what the man is saying, that scared me, and I quickly hung up the phone and I said God! "if what this man is saying is true, reveal it to me and let me understand it, and immediately I was caught up in the spirit, of what seem to be about an hour, but I found out later that it was only five minutes when I called Brother Stokes back and told him that God had revealed everything to me that he was saying to be true. Brother Stokes was overwhelmed with joy. The devil does not want you or me to come into the knowledge of the truth of eternal life. He don't want anybody to overcome death, because death is of the devil, therefore God have a purpose for me to write this book, Jesus cannot lie and all his promises are true. If you keep his sayings you will never die. I don't know anybody of the traditional churches who are preaching the full and complete gospel of Jesus Christ, although they say they are; they praise him and talk about him and his goodness and his power, but they don't keep or talk about his sayings, you can talk about Jesus all day long and refuse to believe his prophecies or the sayings of Jesus and still die. His sayings are his gospel, some might try to simplify what he said but his words does not need to be simplified, they are already simple, he said my way is so plain that a fool can't error, the words that Jesus preached mean exactly what he said, they are not parables. When he said you shall never die or repent that ye might live, he was not speaking parables. Those were his sayings and his truth.

What will happen to your spirit as a confessed believer if you die? Your spirit will return back to God who gave it as he said it would. What will happen to the sinner's spirit when they die? If you will notice I didn't say if they die, because it's a known fact that everyone who does not come to repentance are sinners and they are going to die, because the wages of sin is death. Their spirit will also return back to God who gave it as God said it would. The same as your spirit; but their spirit will be in eternal damnation. Your spirit will be tormented in the presence of God and his holy angels until you love hearing the truth of his word that you don't want to hear now. The truth is torturing when you don't want to hear it, especially when it's nothing you can do about it, if you don't want to hear the truth now, you won't want to hear it than. You are going to be tormented both day and night until you believe and love all of his sayings and fall to your spiritual knees and confess the truth of his word, as he said in the scripture, every knee shall bow and every tongue shall confess. If you are one who have believed in your heart and confessed with your month that Jesus Christ is the son of God and you die, your spirit shall be saved, but the sinner who have never believed nor confessed Jesus Christ to be the Son of God, when he die his spirit will not be saved, he will remain in eternal damnation which mean eternal death. You who have confessed the Lord Jesus Christ to be the son of God and you die for the lack of knowledge or understanding or you didn't keep his sayings: When you hear the truth and understanding of his word your spirit will finally be reconciled to God. Those who overcome death and remain alive, your mortal body shall be changed from mortal to immortality, which mean your mortal body will become spirit.

Somebody said to me one day, if I die I won't know I am dead. That doesn't matter, your spirit is the eternal part of you and your spirit will know that it has left your body and that you are dead. Your body won't know you are dead, because there is no knowledge in the grave. Your spirit will know you are dead, if you die. That will mean you didn't get eternal life because your natural life is ended. To die means an ended life and an ended life can't be called eternal life. When your mortal body die it is no longer mortal, it is corrupted. You are not perfect like God is perfect, therefore your corrupt body can't be change from corruption to immortality because your body is dead and corrupted and no longer mortal. If you have believed in your heart and confessed with your mouth the Lord Jesus, although your body is dead your spirit shall be saved, your reward won't be the same as an overcomer of death. Overcoming death is the glory part of you. It is the perfection of you. That was the purpose for Jesus dying that your body will live and also be glorified as his body was glorified. If you have believed in your heart and confessed with your mouth the Lord Jesus Christ and that God has raised him from the dead, you shall be saved. (Romans 10:9) If you have not blasphemed against the Holy Ghost, your spirit shall be saved in the life to come, But he that shall blaspheme against the Holy Ghost hath never forgiveness, but is in danger of eternal damnation, (Mark 3:29) which means eternal death.

There are many mysteries of God in this book. There are many mysteries that God has revealed to me. Even mysteries that have been hidden from ages to ages and from generations to generations that God said he is revealing to his saints today. (Col.1:26).It is a mystery that people don't know that many scriptures have been removed from the bible by those unbelievers who destroyed and burned the bibles, scriptures that pertains to eternal life, that they might deceive the people of God to cause them to die and not live.

But he that soweth to the Spirit shall of the Spirit reap life everlasting. And let us not be weary in well doing, for in due season we shall reap, if we faint not. (Gal.6:9). Death won't be a common thing in the churches if you will start preaching life instead of death and don't stop preaching life even if somebody dies, finally there will be less and less deaths in the church and people will start living longer diseased free lives and many will remain alive. It will take a while to bring the church out of the doctrine of death, which is the doctrine that man was preaching long before your time and has continued preaching it even until now. It didn't get this way overnight, it took many centuries of preaching the death and brain washing messages that causing the people of God to die, though they don't realize that they are being death indoctrinated and you can't make them believe it. I know because I was there, I was taught the same death messages that you are taught, but God opened the eyes of my understanding and told me to come out from among them. It's on the same order of being on a drug. You have to leave it alone. You can't detox yourself of the doctrine of death until you stop listening to it. That's why God told me that I can't continue to hear the preachers preach the message of death and the Holy Spirit preach life and attain unto life. That's exactly how he said it and told me to come out from among them and be separated. I had to leave it alone. I believe I'm just about detoxed of the death teaching that is causing the people of God to die. It's a known fact that sinners are going to die, because the wages of sin is death, and death is your paycheck for sinning: Gods people should live and not die, so turn yourselves and live.

Your salvation is an individual affair. You can't judge another. Only God can judge weather a person ways have pleased him. When a person die you can't say I know that person lived a good and perfect life and then ask the question and say, well why did he die? Maybe he died for reasons that you don't know about, you don't know how good that person have been in his or her heart with God, or how much they believed; you only know your heart and how real you have been and how much faith you have had with God. Neither can you say, I know he was a sinner because of such and such; what you are calling sin might not mean nothing to God, therefore man looks on the outward appearance but God looks at the heart, only you and God know how real you are with him. Work out your own salvation with fear and trembling; (Phil.2:12) keep preaching what Jesus preached and let the Holy Spirit have his course. The Scripture said, let us not be weary in well doing: for in due season we shall reap, if we faint not;

(Gal 6:9) keep the faith and in due season you will see the results. Jesus word is truth. He said if a man will keep my sayings which are his prophecies he shall never see death; (John 8:51) what Jesus was saying, if you will preach the gospel that I preached, if you will say and believe what I said, you shall never die. It doesn't matter what you think Peter or Paul said, Jesus is telling us to say what he said. Jesus gospel is the only gospel that attain unto life. Men are ashamed to preach the gospel of Jesus Christ. They don't believe it because people are dying every day.

Life was the good news that Jesus came preaching: that through his gospel he brought life and immortality to light. The gospel of Jesus Christ is and should be considered the chief gospel of all the gospels. For your enlightenment, Apostles Paul preached the sayings that Jesus preached about, if a man keep my saying he shall never see death. Or Jesus died that you might live. That's why Paul could say, I'm not ashamed of the gospel of Christ, because he preached that same gospel. Preachers of today don't preach the full gospel of Jesus. They don't even know why Paul said that he's not ashamed. Paul could say he's not ashamed of the gospel of Jesus Christ because he preached those scriptures that you never talk about. The truth is you are ashamed to preach the scriptures that Jesus preached. Therefore you are not preaching the full gospel of Jesus Christ. You have preached death to Gods people. It is not easy to detox yourself of the doctrine of death, I know because I have struggled and are still endeavoring to totally detox myself. I press toward the mark of the high calling of Jesus Christ. (Ph.3:14) Death indoctrination is like a brain washing situation because all you have heard all your life is get saved so you will be ready to die or get saved so when you die, you will go to heaven. Jesus never said get saved to die, he came to save you from death. He said repent and live. It would be a big boost to our eternal life if the church would just lose the phase when you die, or even just the word die, it would be a good thing, if the preachers and teachers would take die completely out of their vocabulary and would only focus on the word live and life. That would help to destroy death more quickly from among God's people. God is not the God of the dead but the living and God is not willing that we be ignorant of such knowledge. By the gospel of Apostle Paul, God let us know that Jesus Christ has abolished death and brought life and immortality to light through the gospel; (2 Tim.1:10) when you start preaching the gospel of Christ and stop preaching death, you will see that the people would have more abundant life. As you come to the light walk in the light.

I believe the reason Methuselah lived 968 years and also others who lived in that time, lived such long lives is because they were not death indoctrinated like people are in the churches today. Enoch was Methuselah's father and Enoch live 365 years and he was translated, (Gen.5:18-32). Enoch was a man who walked with God and by faith he was translated that he should not see death and he was not found because God had translated him: for before his translation he had this testimony that he pleased God. (Heb.11:5-6). But without faith it is impossible to please him: for him that cometh to God must believe that he is, and that he is a rewarder of them who diligently seek him. You must believe and seek to know God in order for this to work for you as it did Enoch, it can only work by faith. Therefore leaving the principles of the doctrine of Christ (which mean leaving the principles of the doctrine of the church; Christ is the church), let us go on unto perfection; (Heb.6:1) (The Holy Spirit spoke these words to me.) "The church can't make you perfect the pastor can't make you perfect, only the Holy Spirit can make you perfect", God want us to know how to be perfect. We must leave the principles of the doctrine of the church and go on to perfection through the gospel of Jesus Christ. I'm not saying leave the church but leave the principles of the doctrine of the church.

UNBELIEVERS BURNED
THE BIBLES

Those unbelievers who burned the bibles in the thirteenth or fourteenth century are the one's who brought about a division of the gospels to cause the church to believe the Apostles gospel to be of a higher authority then the gospel of Jesus Christ. I believe because of what Apostle Paul said, if any man come preaching another gospel than what we preach let him be a curse, but what they don't know is that the Apostle Paul preached Jesus sayings. I use to hear preachers quote that scripture, I am not ashamed of the gospel of Christ, yet I have never heard them quote certain scriptures that Jesus quoted and they never talk about or use those certain scriptures in a sermon from Jesus sayings, that would be the only way to show himself and everybody else that he's not ashamed of the gospel of Christ. Let this book be a wakeup call for all the preachers and teachers whom God have entrusted his word to: start seeking God for the truth of eternal life.

It seem to me that the preachers are all practically preaching and saying what they heard the Reverend or

Doctor So and So preached, more than what the scripture said that Jesus preached, all because Doctor So and So had a degree from such and such bible college, but the question is, what did Doctor So and So get from the Holy Spirit?. When I was a child and also a very young woman, I thought when they said I am not ashamed of the gospel, they meant we were not ashamed of the way we would worship and praise God by shouting and dancing and speaking in tongue and calling on the name of Jesus which only made us a peculiar people in the eyes of the world, because even at that time they didn't preach Jesus sayings, but now that I think about it, what we were doing had nothing to do with being ashamed of the gospel of Jesus Christ. If those things that we did were the gospel, why is that gospel which is supported by scriptures that are found mostly in the New Testament so strange and scary to the people? Many church people get fighting mad when you talk to them about those scriptures, scriptures like (St, John 8:51).will cause many to leave your church, but that's alright, you need to deliver your own soul by preaching and keeping his saying. Though many will say that you have left the faith, the reason many people of the church will say you have left the faith is because they have never heard the real gospel of Jesus Christ preached although they think they have. That's why many church people are so fearful and get so angry when they hear you talk about Jesus sayings, because all they have heard preached is what is said to be the apostle's gospel, but most people have not heard the full gospel of Jesus Christ preached, although they think they have. They honor him with their mouth and mention the name of Jesus and talk about him and talk about what he did for them in every message or testimony that they preach and or give, but they never say what he said about keeping his sayings and what he said about you shall never die.

That's the way the church people feel about Jesus sayings, I believe that they think his saying are parables, because they don't realize that his sayings are his gospel. Keeping his sayings is the only thing that can keep you alive. When you say I am not ashamed of the gospel of Jesus Christ, it is not true, if it were true you would be preaching and teaching every scripture and every word of Jesus saying, like in (John 8:51) if a man keep my saying he shall never die or he shall never see death and Jesus died that we might live. Preaching the fullness of the gospel of Jesus Christ is what made certain people because of fear, jump up and run out of the church when they heard me preach from those scriptures that they never talked about or never heard talked about, as if though, I had just planted those scriptures in the bible. It was the preaching of the gospel of Jesus Christ that caused those unbelievers to burn the bibles in the thirteenth or fourteenth century and even before then. In the rewriting of the bible when they wrote what Paul said: But though we, or an angel from heaven, come preaching any other gospel unto you than that which we preached unto you, let him be a curse. (Gal.1:8) By man reading that and not seeking God by the Holy Spirit for the revelation of that scripture or neither doing research, has caused people to be confused and has brought about a division between the gospel of Apostles Paul and the gospel of Jesus. Seem as though the church believe that the apostle Paul gospel is of a higher authority then the gospel of Jesus; although they won't tell you that, but you know that from the way they preach and teach. Beside all of that, the way the unbelievers burned and also removed scriptures from the bible pertaining to eternal life, that they didn't want you to know. And in the rewriting the bible, the scriptures they took out changed the context of the scriptures, especially the gospels of the apostles and the gospel of Christ. God allowed this to happen in order that the Holy Ghost might have his course in those who are the true believers and the true worshippers of God. But the Anointing; which is the (Holy Ghost) which you have received of him abide in you and you need not that any man teach you, but as the same anointing teaches you of all things, and is truth, and is no lie, and even as it hath taught you, you shall abide in him. (1 John 2:27) Jesus said, he that has ears to hear, let him hear, (Matt.11:15).

For I have no pleasure in the death of him that die said the Lord God: wherefore turn yourselves and live ye: (Ezekiel 18:31-32). God said he have no pleasure in the death of him that die. That meant that God has a plan and a way for you not to die. You might say if that is so "why is everybody dying? Those who are called believers are dying because of unbelief and the spiritual food they are being fed in the churches. Also they die for the lack of knowledge. Pay attention to how: (John 3:16) is read: It is the most common read scripture that everybody reads: <u>For God so loved the world that he gave his only begotten Son that whosoever believeth in him (should not perish or die) but have ever lasting life</u>: I have heard people read that scripture forever, all of my life and they always miss quote it. They never notice how it is read: <u>if you believe in him (you should not perish)</u>. But they always say you shall not perish, it didn't say, you shall not perish. It says if you believe in Jesus, you should not perish (die) if you should not die, what are you going to do about it, the choice is yours.

God said my people are destroyed (die) for the lack of knowledge; you die for the lack of knowledge. (Hosea 4:6). Destroyed mean death. The way we are taught in the churches the born again believers think they already have that knowledge that God is talking about, just because they have been born again, but you don't have that knowledge. You must seek to have the knowledge of God. What you have is your own little knowledge of him. When you began to seek to know him he will began to pour his knowledge into you, than you will have the knowledge of God. Our little knowledge of him is no match for death, the power to overcome death, is the knowledge of God. I know you have heard that knowledge is power. You can know about a person without knowing that person, that's the way it is with us and God. We know about him, we know what he can do, we even know things that he has done for us and in us and through us, we even know who he is, but we don't know him until he reveals himself to us, by revealing his knowledge to us. I will say it again that knowledge is power. There is no power but of God. God said that his people perish for the lack of knowledge.

The church continues to be death indoctrinated by men saying come and get saved or accept the Lord Jesus so you'll be ready to die. Not only are they death indoctrinating you, they are condemning you to death when they say to you, repent and get saved so when you (die). Jesus did not death indoctrinate us neither did he condemn us. Jesus taught us to repent and live. Most people are so deceived and blind even though they hear the preacher say get saved so when you die you will go to heaven, plus, you yourself will say, ("when I die I know I am going to heaven") and then you will turn right around and say, ("yeah, but we don't die"), Dah!!!??. Either you die or you don't die, what's it going to be? When God made me come out of the church, he told me why, he said that I can't continue to hear the preachers preach the message of death and the Holy Spirit preach life and attain unto life. I don't tell people to come out of the church neither do I try to encourage them to come out. I leave that to God. But what God really want, is not for you to come out of the church, but for the preachers to stop preaching death to the church and start preaching life. Preaching life is the gospel of Jesus Christ. I never said that the church is not a blessing to people; it is a blessing to people in multiple ways. I thank God for the church. Me and my children was blessed and healed many times over and over again and we received many miracles while I was going to church. My son Holbert was born with deform legs and a right club foot; what is called bow legs and club feet, his knees stood out like a bow of an arrow and his right foot was turned in and I did nothing because I didn't know what to do. People started talking about him. When he was about seven years old I began to feel guilty that I had neglected my child. I took him to the doctor and ask how can I get my son's legs straighten and the doctor said to me in a scolding tone of voice, "you won't get them straighten!, they will have to be broken 6 or 7 times and reset and they still won't be straight" and he ended by saying, "he will never play football" I got up and took my baby by the hand and I said to myself, you will never brake my baby's legs. My heart was so heavy, I felt sick. I couldn't wait to go to church on Sunday to give it to God. When the prayer line was called, I took my son up for prayer and the Pastor said to me, what do you wanted the Lord to do?, and I was too a shame to say; because I felt I had neglected my child, so I said I have an unspoken request, the pastor who was Elder James Starr said, "God hear unspoken request too", and he prayed, on my way back to my seat I said God you take it! Because I can't handle it, and from that moment on I totally forgot about it and I never thought about it again until he was 16 years old, he was getting ready to go to football practice and the Holy Spirit said, "Look at Holbert's legs" and I said, ooh my God, when did his legs straighten out? I looked at a picture of him at 9 years old and his legs were straight,

God must have healed him instantly I don't know, but God healed him and straighten his legs and foot out. God is so awesome, Holbert played Pro Football for about a year for the Canadian Blue Bombers, his position was, Corner Back, and they wanted him because he was good! But he wanted to come back to the States and God had other plans for him. People go to church for many reasons. Some goes to fine help, hope and healings, many goes to church to fine peace and joy and they fine all of those things and more. But after they find all of those blessings, in the end they die and it should not be that way. I am talking about eternal life and the gospel of Jesus Christ. The gospel of Jesus Christ and your faith is what saves you from death and gives you eternal life. Without faith and the gospel Jesus Christ, people will continue to die. That's because the church continue to be death indoctrinated by the preachers. Jesus said that he died that you might live. He died that your physical body might live. That has absolutely nothing to do with the blessings and the miracles that you received from him in the church. Because the blessings and the miracles that you receive from him just goes to show you that God keep his promises to you if you trust him. He will also keep the same promise of eternal life that he promised that you shall receive of him. If you believe and keep his sayings, you shall never see death.

EXCEPT YOU REPENT
YOU WILL PERISH

Jesus was preaching repentance to some people who told him about the Galileans blood that Pilate had mingled with their sacrifices. Jesus answering and said unto them, you suppose that these Galileans were sinners above all sinners, because they suffered such things?" Jesus said "nay, but accept you repent you shall all likewise perish" (Luke 13:1-5), which meant each of you are going to die same as they died if you don't repent and believe his sayings. Repent is one of Jesus sayings, you have to repent in order to live. You can't repent with the expectation of dying to go to heaven you have to repent with the expectation to live. Jesus said, repent therefore and live. The bible said so a man think so he is, if you think that you are repenting to die that's what you are going to do is die. Jesus said that he died that you might live. Jesus is saying if you believe his sayings you shall live. But if you don't believe you are damned already. : But he that believe not shall be damned (Mark 16:16); if you don't believe you are already dead. There are many who think they were born to die. Jesus came and died to redeem you from death. When people ask the question, what about the born again Christian who die? God said he is not pleased with his people dying and he said that he have no pleasure in the death of him that die, he said to turn you and live. (Ezekiel 18:32).

Many do not seek to know God neither are they taught to seek to know him. They think they already know him. If you say to most church people that God want you to seek to know him. They will tell you I already know him, when I got saved I know him, when he healed me I know him, that's not knowing God, that's knowing about God and knowing what he can do. You must seek to know him in order to know him. For an example, seek to know him by asking him if something is true; concerning eternal life or maybe concerning been made perfect while you live. Since all you ever heard the preachers say is, God knows you can't be perfect. You already know that God can't lie. Why would he say be perfect if it was something you can't do? Now would be a good time to start seeking God for answers on how to be perfect. He will let you know. He let me know. That's how you get to know God, is by seeking to know spiritual things that you think is impossible. Just ask God to reveal it to you and let you understand it. If God said it, believe it.

You must be born again. I believe the Spirit of God can be in you and Christ not yet be birthed in you. He will birth himself in you, as he did in me when I accepted sonship and became a son of God. When I became a son of God I felt something turn over in my stomach with a moving sensation, it is a mystery. It felt like a baby moving and as I felt that movement, I heard the Holy Spirit say, Christ is now birth in you. The scripture said: But as many as received him, to them he gave power to become the sons of God, even to them that believe on his name. (St John 1:12). These sons and this birth were not by the will of man but by the will of God. (St John 1:13) These are some of the mysteries of God. It's just that easy to become a son of God. Even those who just believe on his name have the power to become a son of God, I'm not saying you will feel the same moving sensation that I felt, because becoming a son of God is done by your faith and by the Holy Spirit.

Condemnation is death: There is therefore now no condemnation to them who are in Christ Jesus: (Roman 8:1). When you are in Christ there is no death in you. When God judge you and find no death in you, then you will live. When a man goes to trial for a crime that he has committed and it is said that he is condemned, their plan is to kill that man, because he was condemned. Condemnation means death. When you say, when I die, you are condemning you own self to death, because you have confessed death and therefore unbelief of life brings about death in you and also you have not the knowledge of God. If you had the knowledge of God you would not be preparing to die.

Therefore thou art inexcusable O man, whosoever thou art: (Roman 2:1)" God said; your ways are not my ways, he also said, your thoughts are not my thoughts, (Isa 55:8) In order to receive the promise of eternal life that God made to you, you must seek to know God. We must have the knowledge of God in order to live. Our own little knowledge that we have of God is no match for death. When we began to seek to know God he will began to pour his knowledge into us. Then shall we know if we follow on to know the Lord: (Hosea 6:3) Death won't be a match for us, when we have the knowledge of God. We will have as much of God's knowledge as we need to combat death. God will measure it out according to our faith and for his purpose in us: Broad is the way that leads to destruction. (That led to death) Because strait is the gate, and narrow is the way, which leaded unto life and few there be that find it.(Matt.7:13-14) Many religious leaders are trying to have the biggest church rather than the truth, what might be a reason why some don't preach the full gospel of Jesus Christ nor keep the sayings of Jesus. However they should start preaching the full gospel of Jesus Christ, even if people leave the church. If you fail to preach the true and warn the people of their sin or their unbelief and they die, their blood will be required at your hands, but if you warn the people and they don't hear, their blood will be on their own hand, (Ezekiel 18:20-24) however if they never hear the gospel of Jesus Christ and his sayings preached they will continue to die.

To overcome death we must walk by faith and not by sight and must be steadfast and unmovable and always abounding in the work of the Lord. (1Cor15:58) the Bible said look not to the right or to the left but look straight ahead. God said that we perish for lack of knowledge. We know that we have knowledge, but it is not the kind of knowledge that God is talking about. Our little knowledge that we have of God is no challenge for death. But as God began to pour his knowledge into us, than we are preparing to overcome death if we follow on to know him. Finally death will be no challenge for us, because we will have the knowledge of God. That's why God tells us to seek to know him. This is a prophetic message that God gave to my former pastor who was a great man of God, and highly anointed of the Lord. I believe the prophecy was given in the early 1970's and I quote, "Life is certain and death is sure, but God has made a way for the believer to come out of death alive" the man of God was on to something big and deep and he knew it, but he didn't build on it nor did he seek God for the revelation of that prophecy, because he thought he had it all. You never have it all. Instead of saying God show me how that is done. God would have shown him how to come out of death and remain alive. After knowing that God has made away for the believer to come of death and live, I believe he could have lived. Same as the saints think today, even myself, I thought when we would seek and received the Holy Ghost we had it all, but you have to continue to seek and never stop seeking the Lord. All through the bible God said seek to know me. He never said seek to be filled with the Holy Ghost, he said receive ye the Holy Ghost and seek to know God. He said my people die for the lack of knowledge, the knowledge of God is the way he has made for the believers to come out of death and live. The death that we have to overcome and live is the natural death that came from the old sinful nature that Adam brought on us. Although Jesus died to take that sinful nature off of us, but the church continue to hold on to it by not believing for the purpose that Jesus died. In order for it to work in us, we have to believe it and receive it. When a believer keep Jesus sayings he will be changed from this mortal to immortality. When a believer die the death, his spirit will be resurrected and he will be reconciled back to God. That prophecy that God gave the man of God was a huge foundation to build on concerning eternal life. The interpretation that God gave to me concerning that prophetic statement was that God has made a way for the believer to come out of that sinful nature of death and live. The scripture said: we were born in sin, which is unbelief. We were shaped in iniquity (Psalms 51:5), (Isaiah 59:2) But your iniquities have separated between you and your God. (Isa.59:2). The wages of sin is death, but the gift of God is eternal life. (Rom.6:23) For God has concluded them all under unbelief that he might have mercy upon us all (Rom.11:32) ;(Gal 3:22) Although we were all concluded in death (which came by sin) but God has made a way for the believers to come out of death and live. We have to seek God in order to know how to do this. Because of the way we have been taught, most of us don't know that we have been death indoctrinated by men who didn't know that they didn't have the knowledge of God.

BE PERFECT EVEN AS
GOD IS PERFECT

Be ye therefore perfect, even as(or just like) your Father which is in heaven is perfect(Matt 5:48); you might not ever be perfect as God, but you can be perfect like God is perfect, it's the knowledge of God that makes you perfect as God is perfect. You can be as perfect by the faith you have and the knowledge that you have received of him. For as much knowledge as it takes to fill you up to the fullness of the knowledge of Jesus Christ unto a (perfect man). (Eph.4:13). This perfection is not about being perfect in the eyes of man, but in the eyes of God. Being perfect is first natural then spiritual. For example I can buy a 1 pound can of coffee and you can buy a three pound can of coffee, my one pound can is just as full as your three pound can, although your 3 pound can is larger than mine, but they are both perfectly full. When we talk about spiritual perfection; man being perfect is not about whose right or whose wrong it's about the knowledge of God that makes you perfect as God is perfect. I have heard some people say we will all be perfect when we die and go to heaven; No death does not make you perfect, death is a curse and how can a curse make you perfect? Neither did God promise you heaven. He said to seek ye the kingdom of God. Jesus said the kingdom of God is at hand. You don't have to die to enter into his kingdom, but you do have to overcome death. Neither did God say that he will make you perfect. He told you to be perfect. That mean you be perfect while you're alive, after you die you can't be anything but dead. Therefore you have to be made perfect while you live by seeking to know God. If you as a believer wait until you die to be made perfect, than the sons of God will be the ones who will have to make you perfect: God revealed this scripture to me when he told me and showed me how to make my son Jerome perfect after he had been dead for three months. God instructed me and gave me this scripture that will support what he told me to do. (Hebrews 11:39-40) This scripture is speaking of the sons of God who had to make perfect the believers who have confessed that Jesus Christ is the son of God, yet he died, for either his life style or for the lack of knowledge therefore he were not made perfect which also caused him to die. That mean that he did not receive the promise of eternal life, because he died and had to be made perfect.(Matt.19:26-Mark10:27)With God all things are possible, a perfect man cannot die; God is perfect and he cannot die; In the 1990's in my earlier minister I remember when I first began to receive the ministry of reconciliation, how the Holy Spirit continue to nag at my spirit, I would hear the other women ministers talk about their calling, some of them had such great ministries of prophesying and that was what I always wanted to do, I wanted to know what my calling was, and I had no idea what my calling would be I was hoping it would be prophesying, about 3 o'clock in the morning I cried out to God: and for some reason I said it in a loud voice; I said, "Lord what is my calling and show me how to use it; show me how to use it; that really got my attention, how did I know it was something that I had to be shown how to use it, only the Holy Spirit knew why I said that, but immediately God said divination, and that scared me and also it offended me, because I always heard that divination was of the devil, so I rebuked that in the name of Jesus and I was offended for the lack of knowledge and understanding. So I said if that's the way he's going to talk I'm not going to ask him nothing else. God told me what my calling was but he didn't tell me how to use it and I wasn't about to ask him how to use it, in fact I left it alone and I didn't tell anybody what had happened and I didn't talk about it. I thought to myself, this is crazy, but I didn't know that God was giving me one of the greatest ministries there ever was; though it is a great responsibility; ministering to the spirits of the dead, but thank God that his mercy endures for even. God was giving me the ministry of reconciliation reconciling the spirits of just men back to God. God never left me without a witness. On three different occasions there were two prophets who didn't know each other, and one of whom I didn't know and had never seen, whose name was Pastor Brannan, A white minister who did not know me, as far as

I know I have never spoken two words to him. However he prophesied to me on two different occasions. I was driving pass this little church one night and decided to stop by and go inside, and there this minister was ministering and prophesying to a long line of woman telling them about their sickness and diseases, I set down for a few minutes, and the Holy Spirit told me to go up and get in the prayer line. I said no, its nothing wrong with me, He said, you go to the doctor for a physical diagnosis, why don't you go up and get a spiritual diagnosis. I had no idea of what it was about but I obeyed and went up and when I approached him, he looked at me and said, Sister there is nothing wrong with you, you have divine health, but God is bringing you into an unusual ministry and then he prayed. That was the 1st time he said to me; Sister God is bringing you into an unusual ministry, the second time was about 5 years later. The devil attacked my teeth with something that I can't see but I can feel a sense of something constantly coming out of my tooth and I am constantly blowing something out of my mouth that I can't see. And lest I should be exhalted above measure by the abundance of the revelations, a thorn in the flesh was given to me, a messenger of Satan to buffet me, lest I be exhalted above measure. (2Cor. 12:7-8). there were given me a thorn in the flesh by the messenger of Satan for the same purpose that was given Apostle Paul, lest I should also be exhalted above measure. It was so annoying, I thought it would drive me crazy, and when it provoked me and I acted in response, then it would attack me with a painful sensation of something sharp piercing into my gum, and I heard the Holy Spirit say, (Abstain) and I did, I had never heard that word spoken before nor since, but I left it alone. I went to the dentist to see what was wrong with my teeth and he found nothing wrong. I insisted on him taking that tooth out, reluctantly he took that good tooth out of my mouth and the problem immediately moved to the next tooth. It seemed to have been driving me crazy. Somebody said it might be witchcraft. When our Distract Convocation started, one night pastor Brannan was there and announced that he would be in charge of the prayer line the next night. I went to church the next night purposely to get in his prayer line and it was a long line. But I was hoping to get a word from the Lord of what was happening to my teeth. When I approached the minister for prayer, he didn't ask me anything, he just said, Sister there is no witchcraft on you, there is no witchcraft in your house, there is no witchcraft nowhere about you, but God is bringing you into an unusual ministry. That was my first time seeing this minister, since five years earlier and I haven't seen him since. Neither have I ever talked with him in my whole life. God gave him to say those same thing to me; "Sister, God is bringing me into an unusual ministry". You would think that he was somebody who knew me, but he didn't know me and I didn't know him: the second was a prophetess whose name was Pastor Doris Davis, she prophesied and said the same identical words that Pastor Brannan said, She said ooh Sister Money, God is brining you into an unusual ministry. These two prophesies came about four years of each other and five years before I ask God, '(What is my calling and show me how to use it)' God told me what my calling was but he didn't show me how to use it until five years later. God used the death of my son to show me how to use my calling. My son Jerome died in 1995, Three months after he died I had a dream about him, that he was cleaning his room, he had moved just about everything out on the balcony and look like his TV was about to fall and I went up to tell him that his TV was about to fall and I couldn't find him because he was hiding from me under the bed. After I woke up I felt really hurt because my son was hiding from me. I started crying because I thought he didn't want to see me. I ask God why my son didn't want to see me and immediately God answered me and said; he didn't want to hear what you had to say. Then God instructed me and said, bind that rebellious spirit and loose Jerome from it, so he can go to the place of perfection that he might be made perfect. I obeyed God and said, you spirit of rebellion, I bind you in the name of Jesus and I loose Jerome from you so that he might go on to the place of perfection to be made perfect. That was how and when God showed me how to use my calling, that he called divination. The purpose of divination is to minister to the spirits of just men. And set them free from the bondage of death. That they might be made perfect Like God is perfect. God's purpose for the Ministry of Reconciliation is to reconcile the Spirit of Just Men back to God as they were before they died. It is not Gods will for anybody to die. Reconciliation can only be done by those who have the ministry of reconciliation. Heb.11:39). When you are dead there is nothing else you can do for yourself. Somebody have to do it for you. That's why God gave the ministry of reconciliation.

God is not the God of the dead but of the living. And it's the knowledge of God that makes you perfect as God is perfect. We always say Lord I want to be like you. If you are going to be like God you have to be perfect like God is perfect. A perfect man cannot die (John 14:19). Jesus said because he lives you shall live also. God gave gifts unto men for the perfecting of the (church) (of the saints) for the work of the ministry, for the edifying of the body of Christ, till we all come into the unity of the faith, (Eph.4:11-13) that doesn't mean everybody will come into the unity of the faith at once. Because your faith is personal and it's not talking about uniting with one another in the faith it's talking about uniting with God in the faith. But as you being a minister with one or more of these gifts you should try to bring as many as you can into the faith and cause them to be unite into the faith of God and in the knowledge of Jesus Christ unto a perfect man. Some people think this is a private journey. When God reveal something to you or tell you something, they think it's just for you. This knowledge of God is too powerful and too great for one individual to try to keep for himself. God don't have a one man's journey. God gives his knowledge to someone who will willing share and is not a shame of sharing it. And one who is not ashamed of the gospel of Jesus Christ. I share it with as many as will listen. You are not going to get everybody, (Matt 25:15, and 25) \But at least you don't bury it or set on it like the man who was given the one talent and buried it. Therefore you deliver yourself by sharing it with as many as will receive it. Bring as many that will listen that they might receive the knowledge of the Son of God unto a perfect man. Until we all come unto the measure of the faith and the stature of the fullness of the knowledge of Jesus Christ. Every inch of your inter most being must be filled with the knowledge of God and of Jesus Christ until you become a perfect man, like God is perfect. God said that he give us pastors according to his own heart who shall feed us with knowledge. But you have to receive that knowledge of God before you can feed knowledge to anybody else. God said if any man think he know anything, he don't know nothing as he ought to know.

Many religious people don't know that they don't have the knowledge of God and many are mostly preaching what they heard other men preach. Some religious people only read the bible and draw their opinion just by reading. You don't get eternal life by reading the bible, unless the Holy Spirit reveal to you what you are reading and the meaning of what you are reading. There are many things in the bible that you don't understand, without the Holy Spirit revealing to you what it mean and what the mind of God was concerning that scripture, even though it seemed to be easy and simple. God said my people die for the lack of knowledge. Unless God open the eyes of the preachers and teachers understanding they don't know what that scripture mean. For the lack of the knowledge of God they are death indoctrinating the church and condemning the people of God and causing them to die. They are not aware when they say, when you (die) they are pronouncing death on you. That's because they are blinded to the truth. I find that some of the people they say it to, claim they have never heard a preacher say get saved or accept the Lord so when you die you'll go to heaven. I know they have heard it. That is one of their scare tactic they use. I always heard it and I still hear it on television. I use to think it was alright when I didn't know I was being death indoctrinated. Most of them don't know they are being death indoctrinated either. Most preachers don't know they are death indoctrinating the people. Because they only know what they have been taught. If you will start seeking God for the answer, he will give it to you.

The old saying that they use to say in the church is that you should never question what the pastor say, there is no scripture to support that and the bible say that you are the captain of your own soul. And work out your own salvation with fear and trembling. (Phil.2:12-16) Another old saying is that you can't be no stronger than your leader, that's true because when you begin to get more knowledge from God then he or she have, they will say you have left the faith or why would God reveal something to you when he can reveal it to the pastor. Sometimes the pastor might not listen to the Holy Spirit. If the Holy Spirit is telling you to seek to know God as he was telling me for three or four years and if you obey him he is going to reveal himself to you as he does to me. If you are seeking to know God and your leader is not seeking to know God; there is a good chance of you having more knowledge of God then he or she have. Two or three time per year the anointing which is the Holy Spirit would come upon me, and under that anointing I would cry and say Lord let me down in the deep secret of your word. I thought I was going crazy. I ask God, why do I keep saying that and what are the deep secrets of his word? For year's every time I got up to speak or bring a message it didn't matter what scripture I read I found myself talking about getting to know God. People of God you need to get to know God by seeking to know him and start paying close attention to what's being said to you from the pulpit and I mean really listening. And start reading scriptures for yourself. Jesus never said when you die, he said repent and live. Some people have told me that they don't want the knowledge of God. What the scripture said about the children of Israel because they didn't desire knowledge therefore he turned them over a reprobated mind so they would rather believe a lie then the truth, (Roman 1:28).

That's why many are spiritually blinded. They rather believe a lie then the true, and because of that, there are so much sickness, diseases and death in the churches. Jesus said that he died that you might live. When they burned the original bible in the thirteenth or the fourteenth century, they put it back together by removing scriptures pertaining to eternal life out of it, to deceive the people of God and to make it look like the apostles taught a different doctrine then Jesus taught and their teaching had more authority then Jesus teaching. That's why the Holy Spirit has to reveal the truth to you and reveal to you what they didn't put back in the bible concerning eternal life, and Jesus teaching and the Apostles teaching; they taught the same things, but that was the unbelievers way of bringing about a division and a deception of the gospel of Jesus Christ, by removing certain scriptures out of the bible. You can see the same kind of deception happening in everyday life, it is happening to our country and all over the world. People are bringing about a division, dividing the people because they don't like certain people who are in authority, though people know the truth yet they listen to lies. If somebody does something to help the people, another group will say things to scare the people to bring about a division that's what they did with Jesus. Jesus said that he died that you might live. Men back in that day changed the truth of God's word into a lie and taught the people that they had to die that graveyard kind of death and called it eternal life. They are still teaching the same thing. If you really think about eternal life it doesn't make sense to die and then call your life eternal. Eternal anything does not change from what it originally is to something else and still be called eternal. If life is life it has to remains life in order to be called eternal life. It can't change from life to death and be called eternal life. Don't let the devil deceive you.

The Bible say to lean not unto your own understanding: (Proverb 3:5). Heaven is God's dwelling place and so does he dwell in the believer. Yes God dwells in the believer. When Jesus said in my Father's house are many mansion, if it were not so, I would have told you. What he is saying is, in my father's house are many (people or saints). I go to prepare a place for you, and if I go and prepare a place for you, I will come again, and receive you unto myself, there where I am, there ye may be also. (John 14:2, 3) He was not talking about physical living quarters or physical mansions or a physical heaven. He was talking spiritually. Talking about the people, the believers like Abraham, Moses and others (BC) whose spirits were already with God. They are the mansions that Jesus was talking about. When Jesus said I go to prepare a place for you. I believe Jesus was talking about us the believer who are alive and who will remain alive. Heaven is God's dwelling place. If he dwells in me or you, we are heaven. Therefore we are his dwelling places. God spoke of heavens, signifying there is more than one. He also spoke of the believers being clothed with their spirit house which shall come down from heaven. The bible speaks of heaven as being Gods dwelling place. Although the believers are also God's dwelling place. I know he dwells in me. Howbeit Jesus did not say he was going away to prepare heaven, he's going away to prepare a place for those who believe in him. If heaven is where God wanted you to be, he would also have made a way for you to get to heaven without dying. He knew the church would be death indoctrinated. God knew that most people who received him would not remain alive, because of the spiritual food that they would be fed, Ye also, as lively stone, are built up a spiritual house an holy priesthood, (1 Peter 2:5) the scripture calls the believer a built up spiritual house and holy priesthood which is equal to a mansion. God called us a royal priesthood. (1Peter 2:9) Royalty qualifies you as a mansion.

God never said you would inherit heaven but you would inherit the earth if you overcome death. (Rev 21:7) God said he have no pleasure in the death of him that die; (Ezek. 18:32). Precious in the sight of the Lord is the death of his saints. (Psalms 116:15). This scripture is talking about the saints who were killed for the sake of the gospel. God call their death precious. They gave their lives for the sake of the gospel of Jesus Christ. God has promised the believers an immortal body without sickness or disease. (Romans 8:13) But we have to believe in order to have it. You have to seek to know God, and the more he reveals himself to you is the more he brings you into his marvelous light and you have to walk in that light in order to overcome death.

Apostle Paul said we shall be changed from this mortal to immortality. You will become total spirit. The redemption of their soul is precious, and it ceased forever, (Psalms 49:8-15). If you die, your soul is lost forever. But your spirit will return back to God who gave it .However your spirit can be saved. Those who keep Jesus saying shall not die. But if you are killed for the sake of the gospel of Jesus Christ your soul shall be redeemed. He should still live-forever, and not see corruption, Jesus was dead and in the grave for three days, which his body did not see corruption. God will redeem the soul of those who gave their life for his sake and of the gospel from the power of death. Redeem mean to buy back or to restore. He didn't promise to redeem the soul of those who died a natural death. He told you to repent and live. You can't just only believe that Jesus Christ is the Son of God, you have to believe the full gospel of Jesus Christ that's found in the four gospels of (Matthew Mark Luke and John) you have to believe every word that comes out of the mouth of God or you will die the death. The gospel according to Apostle Paul, said we shall be changed from this mortal to immortality. In this mortal house we groan, we have pain, sickness, and diseases, but in our Spirit house which is of GOD and is come down from heaven, not in heaven; in this house from heaven there is no pain, no sickness and no death.

We know that we are now clothes upon with our earthly house, which is our mortal house, for in this house we groan, earnestly desiring to be clothed upon with our spiritual house which is from heaven. GOD will send our spiritual house from heaven. (2 Cor.5: 1), which will be our immortal house. We will not be changed by death but by Spirit and we will live eternally in our Spirit house.

We shall inherit all things. That means the earth, he didn't say heaven; we will inherit the earth when we are changed from this mortal body to immortality. We will become total spirit, in a moment in the twinkling of an eye.

(1 Cor.5:52). It is a mystery. We only know what the scripture said and what the Holy Spirit reveals to us. Actually when you read the scriptures they say nothing about going to heaven, lest knowing dying and going to heaven. The only scripture that speaks of going to heaven said, "And no man hath ascended up to heaven, but he that came down from heaven; (St. John 3:13). And that was Jesus who ascended up to heaven and who descended down from heaven. Most people don't know that nobody else have gone up to heaven, because the preachers don't preach it and most people don't read the scriptures for themselves, neither do they read with an understanding, nor do they pray for an understanding. If they do read and understand the scripture they will think to themselves that the pastor don't talk about this scripture so it must not be important or it mean such and such, so I have to believe the pastor more than what that scripture say. I know because I did the same thing for years. I'm not telling anybody not to listen to your pastor but read the scripture for yourself. You see what the scripture is saying. I have heard those who only listen to what the pastor say or to what man say. They will say yeah but we don't die, we go to sleep, sleep and dead can mean the same thing. When Lazarus died Jesus said I have to go and wake Lazarus, he sleep. Those who was with him said Master if he sleep he does well. Then Jesus said Lazarus is dead. (John 11:11). He was not talking about a restful sleep, he was talking about death. Jesus has not promised to awake you out of the sleep

that you are talking about or like he did Lazarus. He had a purpose for awakening Lazarus out of death.

Jesus told you to repent and live and not to go to sleep. The only people who are legally put in the grave are dead people. That is where Jesus was when he was dead. He was in the grave for three days. He said he was in hell (yes the grave is hell). He was preaching to the spirits of people who died on the other side of the flood. Jesus called the grave hell. Most people don't know that hell is the grave. They think hell is a lake of fire some place on the back side of yonder. Jesus said if your right hand offends thee, cut it off and cast it from thee: for it is profitable for thee that one of thy members should perish, (die) and not that thy whole body should be cast into hell (grave). (Matt 5:30) Paul said let us not sleep as others sleep. Evidently Paul knew what religious people would be calling death; when he said let us not sleep as others sleep. (1Thes. 5:6) Many scriptures are written plain and clearly, even without the help and revealing of the Holy Spirit; much of man's teaching is not even found in the bible, like dying and going to heaven is not in the bible. Many people get the bible and gather lot of scriptures. That's what we call running references or homiletics, they read those scriptures and bring them together and make them say what they want them to say and that's the way most preachers get their answers and their messages which is very risky without the revealing of the Holy Spirit. Jesus words are plain and they are truth. He say exactly what he mean unless he is talking in parables and if he's talking in parable he always said, hear ye a parable. Jesus said my people perish for lack of understanding. Jesus also said that "my way is so plain that a fool can't error. I don't have anything against running references or homiletics, but you are asking for trouble when you overlook what Jesus said. What Jesus said are the prophecies that the angel of the Lord talks about. Jesus tells us that if you add to or take away from the prophecies of this book which are Jesus sayings, he will take your name out of the book of life and if you add to these prophecies, he will add the plagues to you that is written in the book, (Rev.22:18-19) plagues of sickness diseases and death, will be added unto you: the scripture said out of all your getting, get an understanding.

BELIEVE OR BE DAMNED

He that believe not shall be damned (Mark 16:16) damned means die. I believe people would be quicker to accept the Lord if they knew that seeking to know him and repentance and turning from their sins could cause them to live. Jesus have already died and bore our sickness and taken away the curse and redeemed us from death. (Gal.3:13-14) It will work for you if you will accept it. Sin is a curse and the wages of sin is death, (Romans 6:23) Why don't the people of God accept what Jesus did and said and live. That would put an end to preparing to die. Jesus died to pay the cost for Adams sins that caused death to come on us. So we won't have to die if we will believe it. When Jesus said to one of his disciples, come and follow me and the disciple reply was, first I have to go and bury my father and Jesus said let the dead bury their dead. (Matt.8:21-22). What Jesus was saying was let the unbelievers bury the unbelievers, unbelievers are called the dead. When you believe and get saved you shouldn't die a natural death. (John 3:15, 16) Jesus said "if you keep my sayings you will never die. He said keep his saying, he didn't say if you keep what you think Peter or

Paul or some other preacher said; unless their sayings were the same as Jesus saying were. Jesus said keep his sayings. If those unbelievers had not burned the original bible and took scriptures out of context, we would see that Paul and Peter were saying the same thing that Jesus said; that's why they lost their lives, because they were preaching what Jesus preached. The entire bible is not there as it were before; but what they took out; made the bible like unto a great and wonderful giant source of foot notes for the believers who are led by the Holy Spirit and to those who walk by faith and not by sight. Most people only believe what they see with their eyes: Jesus said blessed is he, who believed without seeing: God allowed the bible to be written in the first place for those who have to see before they believe. God said there will come a time that the word will be written on the tables of your heart and not on tables of stones.(2 Cor.3:2-3) That's why God gave his Holy Spirit to us, that He will teach us and lead us in all the ways of the truth.(1 John.2:27).

When you began to seek to know God he will began to reveal all things to you, even scriptures that have been removed out of the bible. That is one of the mysteries of God. It is a mystery because most people don't know that scripture have been removed out of the bible: they are also termed as mysteries because they have been removed and yet the Holy Spirit reveals them to the believer. People think that God should set watch over the bible that they call God's word, so it will be safe; God's word is safe, because of the revealing of the Holy Spirit. When the Holy Spirit reveals something to you, it's the truth and no lies, you shall abide in that. (John 2:27) Jesus never made it easy for unbelievers to know the truth, that's why he spoke to them in parables. Peter asked Jesus, Master why do you speak to the people in parables? Jesus said it's not for them to know the truth; it's for you to know. When God began to reveal these truths to you, the people in the churches will say you have left the faith, because you have knowledge that they don't have. That's because they do not seek to know God. Search the scriptures for in them you think you have eternal life and they are they who testify of me; (John 5:39) most people who testify of Jesus Christ think they have eternal life, even though they die. They are deceived for the lack of knowledge. They don't seek to know God and many read and read and read and they are never able to come into the knowledge of the truth. God who also made us able ministers of the New Testament and not of the letter, but of the spirit: for the letter kills, but the spirit give life, (2 Cor. 3: 6) The bible is the letter that will kill you unless you let the Holy Spirit reveal to you the knowledge that are hidden in the scriptures that you are reading.

EZEKIEL WAS A PROPHET

Ezekiel was a prophet and the prophetic words that he prophesied then, stands good for today. The Lord said if you fail to warn the people and tell them of their sins, (of their unbelief) they will die and their blood will be required at your hand. Jesus said repent you therefore and live, he said, except you repent you will likewise die. If you fail to tell the people what Jesus said, they will die and their blood will be required at your hand. God entrusted his word to you to teach the people, if you teach them the truth of God's word and they consider and repent of their sins, they shall live. If they don't repent of their sins they shall die and not live, but you will have delivered your own soul. Sin is the reason you die, for the wages of sin is death. Some of the criticism I have experienced of trying to overcome death, is not preparing to die as the world think I should be doing. When you do what the world is doing you are not walking by faith. When you are walking by faith the devil will try to wear you out day and night with the thoughts of why you should prepare to die. To walk by faith you must totally believe Jesus saying and stand on them. Jesus said if any man keeps my sayings he shall never see death. The bible say build up your most Holy faith by praying in the Holy Ghost. You have to do a lot of praying in tongue, which is praying in the Holy Ghost and that is what I do to confirm and reconfirm my faith. You can't prepare to die and live. You must have total faith in what Jesus say.

THE CHALLENGES OF
OVERCOMING DEATH

Think about it. If you believe in Jesus why are you preparing to die? Jesus said that he died that you might live. If you don't believe Jesus sayings, according to scripture you are damned (dead) already. The scripture said: For God so loved the world that he gave his only begotten Son who so ever believeth in him should not die, but have everlasting life; (John 3:16) People get the wrong understanding about everlasting life and resurrection. I want to make clear the meaning, one must be dead naturally or spiritually in order for one to be resurrected and you must be alive and remain alive in order to call your life everlasting life or eternal life. Eternal anything is a continuation of what it currently is. If life is life it must remain life in order to be called Eternal Life. I believe the strategic of overcoming death and attaining unto Life is belief and keeping Jesus sayings.

You shall receive power after the Holy Ghost is come upon you.(Acts 1:8) Pray without ceasing, love your neighbor as you love yourself and love God with all your heart. Do well to your enemy, govern yourself. Bring yourself under subjection. Do not try to lead and govern others and you have not governed your own self. Getting saved do not make you perfect, it is the foundation you build on to be perfect.

Jesus said, Enter ye in at the strait gate; for wide is the gate, and broad is the way, that leaded to destruction, and many there be which go there in. (Matthew 7:13-14) destruction mean death. Because strait is the gate, and narrow is the way which leaded unto life, and few there be that find it. According to what Jesus said, these ingredients and challenges should be easy. Jesus said, my yoke is easy and my burdens are light, (Matthew 11:30). Paul said, not as though I had already attained, either were already perfect, but I follow after, if that I may apprehend that for which also I am apprehended of Jesus Christ, (Phil.3:12-16) neither do I count myself to have attained eternal life but I am pressing toward the mark of the high calling of Jesus Christ that I may overcome death and attain Eternal Life.

SUPPORTING SCRIPTURES

The soul that sin, it shall die. When a righteous man turned away from his righteousness, and committed iniquity, and die in them for his iniquity that he hath done he shall die, again, when the wicked man turned away from his wickedness that he has committed, and do that which is lawful and right, he shall save his soul alive. (Ezekiel 18:20, 26-29). To be saved alive mean to live. Religious people believe that being saved mean you are ready to die and go heaven which is false teaching. Being saved mean that you are ready to live, it mean to be saved from death and live. Notice the scripture said: (he shall save his soul alive) he considered, and turned away from all his transgressions that he had committed, he shall surely live, he shall not die, repent, and turn yourselves from all your transgressions, so iniquity shall not be your ruin. Cast away from you all your transgressions whereby you have transgressed and make you a new heart and a new spirit, for why will you die o house of Israel? For I have no pleasure in the death of him that die said the Lord God, wherefore turn yourselves and live ye.

BY REVELATION

By revelation, I received scripture that is no longer in the bible, but they have been removed. According to the revelation that I received, those two scriptures were located in the book of (<u>Luke 13th chapter</u>), about the 6 and or 7th verse, they were Jesus gospel and his sayings, written in red ink from the gospel of Luke, the 1st verse were, "Repent ye therefore that ye might live; 2nd verse were, "Repent ye therefore that you and your children might live." I read those scriptures about three or four different times within a period of a week. When I got ready to record the verse number of the scriptures in my book, they had disappeared. They were nowhere to be found. The Holy Spirit let me know that they were scriptures that had been removed out of the bible: when the bibles were destroyed and burned. They were not allowed to be put them back in the bible when it was rewritten. The bible speaks of mysteries that's been hidden from ages to ages and from generation to generations that God is revealing to his saints today, (Col 1:26) To receive scriptures by revelation that has been taken out of the bible centuries ago, certainly is a mystery. But the anointing which you have received of him abide in you, ye need not that any man teach you: but as the (Holy Ghost) which is the anointing, teaches you of all things, and is truth and is no lie, and as it hath taught you, ye shall abide in him, (1st John 2:27) the Holy Spirit will lead and guide you in all the way of the truth.

The original bibles was destroyed and burned in the 13th or 14th Century. And was later rewritten, by King James and others; That's why my bible is called the King James Version, according to history it's not the original bible, it is his version of the bible. The Holy Spirit revealed to me that they didn't change the reading of scriptures, but they removed scriptures out of the bible that they didn't want you to know; scriptures like what happened to Mary the mother of Jesus and other followers of Jesus who's name were mentioned in the bible. My inquiry is, what happened to those people did they die a natural death? Or were they killed? Or were they changed from mortal to immortality? The holy bible that we read does not give account of what happened to them. It give account of some of those who were killed for the sake of the gospel of Christ; like Paul, Peter, John the Baptist and Steven; but Mary the mother of Jesus and the others followers of Jesus. Why doesn't it give account of what happened to them especially the mother of Jesus? It seems as if she had died that should have been just what those unbelievers wanted, so they could say that

Jesus was a false prophet. That would have been the biggest headline news in the whole creation. I can just see the big headlines flashing lights and the joy of those who didn't believe in Jesus and his teaching of eternal life. Those unbelievers would have said, see!! I told you that Jesus was a fake! And that his teaching of eternal life was false, which would have been true if Mary his mother and his followers had died a natural death. They would have said "His own mother who believed in him is dead" my answer is that Mary and those who believed and followed Jesus did not die. I believe they remained a live as Jesus said they would. I believe they were transformed into spirit. In the 13th or the 14th century I believe some believers were still keeping Jesus sayings. When they burned the original bible and burned those people at the stake to stop the kind of teaching that Jesus taught. It was nothing but politics, same as it is today, it's was all about money and the rich. Can you imagine what would happen to the mortuaries if only the believers would stop dying? They would go bankrupted. I believe there are more people who confessed that Jesus Christ is the son of God than not. Subsequently some scriptures have been removed, which changed the context of the bible. Nevertheless the bible is still the most powerful book in the world. There is no book equivalent to it. However it behooves us to pray and seek God for the revelation knowledge of scriptures and to wait on God for the answer: as the Holy Ghost (the anointing) that is abiding in you, reveals something to you, it's the truth and is no lie, even as it has taught you, you shall abide in the Holy Ghost teaching.

THERE IS A WAY WHICH SEEMETH RIGHT

There is a way which seem right unto a man, but the end there of is the ways of death. Nobody wants to die. If people wanted to die they wouldn't go to the doctor, they wouldn't fly from all over the world to those healing revivals trying to get healed and many are healed. I have been healed many times all my life even as a child, my father would pray for his children and instantly God would heal us, my mother and father said when I was eleven month old I had double pneumonia and died, I stopped breathing, my dad picked me up and took me in the kitchen and closed the door behind him and started praying for me and he said I started back to breathing. My father's manners were after he prayed for you he would feed you if you haven't been eating food. I hadn't been eating and he fed me. God instantly healed me, and the next morning they said I was up playing with the other children. I have had two death experiences and have had several near death experiences. I set in the church one Sunday morning and died, I was not sick. God gave me my life back. The purpose for me dying that Sunday morning was because I told God that our church needed a miracle and I said oh no, not for me because I know what you can do, but for the sake of the people give our church a miracle. This was on Tuesday night, something was said by the new pastor, that I thought he should not have said; he said there was no such thing as healing and that bothered me. That was why I told God that our church needed a miracle. Be careful what you ask for. Afterward I realized, if it wasn't for me why shouldn't it be me?: This is one of the near death experiences I had. My husband Elder Hayward High and I were coming home from the Holy Convocation in Memphis, Tenn. I was driving late at night, going about 85 miles per hour trying to find a resting area, and I fell asleep. What woke me up; I heard a loud excited voice crying out, Harrison Ross!, Harrison Ross!, Harrison Ross!, Satan was calling out to Harrison Ross the funeral home, he was so excited because he thought he had me, he thought I would die in a car crash and he got so excited, that's why he was calling out to Harrison Ross. It was not his purpose to wake me up but his purpose was to kill me. But God was with me and allow the devil to call out with excitement to wake me up. The devil knew God's purpose for me is to live and not die. The thief cometh not but to steal and to kill, and to destroy (John 10:10)

My husband died of pancreas cancer and at the same time that he was sick I had the same symptoms that he had, though I didn't tell anybody and I didn't go to the doctor.

Evangelist Bennie M Hicks and I ask my husband Pastor Hayward High for a revival and he told us to set it up; the night of the revival I had lost my voice and I couldn't speak above a whisper; therefore Evangelist Hicks had to start the revival off. Here I was standing up in support of her. She stop in the mist of her message and pointed her finger at my stomach and said, I rebuke that cancer in the name of Jesus; instantly I felt a thump in my stomach and all that condition went away. I was healed. God healed me. I hadn't told anybody how I was feeling or what I was going through. I didn't have a Doctor's diagnosis. The Holy Spirit said cancer and the Holy Spirit can't lie. I am a three times cancer survivor. The devil has always tried to kill me one way or another. God's purpose for me is to live and not die. It is God who healeth all our diseases. (Psalms 103:3)God said it's not his will that any should perish. If you have unbelief in you, then there is no hope for you to live. (Matthew 18:14) Jesus said except you repent you will likewise perish. I often hear people say. I will be healed if it's the Lords will or if I die I am ready to go to heaven. If you are a believer and trying to please the Lord, it is Gods will for you to be healed. Sometime when a person is sick God is trying to get their attention in order to get them to a place in him that being sick will cause you to seek after the Lord, and get down to business with God. He might not heal you until you do what he want you to do. I say that because God told me not to ask him to heal me anymore, he said as I pray for others I'll be healed.

He is doing just that, he is healing me of my diseases. He has healed me of osteoporosis which is a bone disease and many other things. From time to time he heals me of something as he said he would as I pray for others. He has not healed me of everything yet. Sometimes he might be chastising you, or trying you, like he did Job. He said it's not his will for you to perish, but if you don't get down to business with God, you will die. Who have delivered us from the authority of darkness: (Colossians 1:13). In case you don't know what perish mean, it means death. God said: I would that you prosper and be in health, even as your soul prosper (3 John 1:2) If you are sick and or have an affliction in your body, the bible said for you to pray and examine yourself to see if you have any un-forgiveness or unbelief in you or something you need to get right. He said take heed to your ways. Pray ye one for another that you might be healed, and if you are sick call for the Elders of the Church. Don't ever be ashamed to ask for prayer. I don't judge anybody, but I know by experience when God keep warning you of something and you don't take heed, he might be allowing something to happen to you or in your body to get your attention. Sometimes what you are doing maybe something that you might think is no harm but if God is not pleased, you had better leave it along. God said that he is a jealous God. You might be spending too much time on the phone or watching television or even with a relative or a friend and not enough time in prayer with God or doing what he is telling you to do.

Sometimes we have to separate ourselves in order to please God. When God want your attention he knows how to get it. He might allow the devil to attack you with something in order to get what he won't. Whom the Lord loveth he chasteneth (Heb.12:6) God touched and healed my knee, but he didn't heal all the problem of one of my knees neither did he heal my hips but as instantly as he healed my knee I heard the Holy Spirit say, "don't ask me to heal you anymore as you pray for others you will be healed" God had allowed the devil to attack me with an arthritis condition in order to make and shape my life and cause me to totally perfect myself in prayer and in my calling: from time to time God heals me of something else as he promised. I am almost healed of everything including arthritis. I am still trying to prefect myself by praying for others. I am not saying everybody who gets sick that God is trying to get your attention. Some sickness is caused by your life style and some just happens. I have an intercessory prayer ministry and also the ministry of reconciliation, reconciling the spirits of just men back to God that they might be made perfect. I intercede for people all over the world. God told me to pray for others and also pray to set the ones who are in captivity free.

The scripture said that all things work together for the good of those who love God and are called according to his purpose. I don't' say that you should thank God for everything that happens to you, but you should thank and praise him in the mist of everything that happens to you. One day I said, "Lord I know that I am in the potter's house," as soon as I said that, I heard the Holy Spirit say, many have died in the potter's house. He was letting me know that just because I am in the potter's house doesn't guarantee that I am coming out of it alive. Coming out alive depends on my sincerity and obedience to God. The potter house is where you are to get totally down to business with God and to prepare yourself for eternal life. Everybody doesn't get totally down to business with God and they die. You have to perfect yourself in order to overcome death and have eternal life. (Jeremiah 18:1-6). God allow you to go into the potter house so he can mold and shape you and perfect you, so you will be able to overcome and put death under your feet. (1 Co 15:26-28, 54-57)Many go in the potter house and never allow God to do what he will with them, if you never get serious with God you will die without getting the victory. The potter's house is where I am right now. I am going through trials and tribulations and trying to please God of whatever he want of me. Weather my family or anybody else understand it or not. I am trying to prepare and perfect myself against that day when death might visit me, that I might be ready. In order for me to overcome and have the victory over death I have to bring myself under subjection by getting totally serious with God. I have to let my words be few and seasoned with grace. You don't have to do anything to die but you do have to do something to live. He didn't say he will make you perfect, he said for you to be perfect. That sounds like something you have to do. I believe that seeking to know God will help you to bring yourself under subjection. You have to have total faith in God and love God with all your heart love your neighbor as you love yourself, do good to your enemy.

THE WAYS OF THE
LORD ARE LIFE

GOD said: "For my thoughts are not your thoughts, neither are my ways your ways said the Lord. My ways are far as the heavens are higher than the earth so are my ways higher than your ways and my thoughts than your thoughts. (Isa 55:8-9)(John 5:39-40) Search the scriptures; for in them ye think ye have Eternal Life and they are they, which testify of me; (v.40) ye will not come to me, that ye might have life. I have had some to tell me that trying to overcome death has been tried before. Even if those who tried it failed or even if I fail: God's word is still true and it cannot fail. If you walk according to his word you will make it. The race is not given to the swift or the battle to the strong. But the one who endure to the end. (Eccl 9:11) You can't quit and win the race you must continue in the race. This is a narrow and tedious journey, according to scripture, only a few will fine this way. For who so ever shall keep the whole law and yet offend in one point, he is guilty of all (James 2:10). This is not the Law of Moses that I'm talking about, this is the sayings of Jesus Christ which you must keep in order to overcome and you can't just keep one of his sayings you must keep them all or you won't make it into the kingdom. You can see why the church is not preaching the sayings of Jesus, because they don't believe them. You have to believe his saying no matter who is dying, his word is true.

I went through an ordeal with Adelanto sheriff dept. with a certain Officer about six years ago, because of a lie that she told, that caused me to lose my section 8 for low income housing. I thought it was totally because of her deception that caused me to lose it, but God had a purpose. God will even use the deeds of an evil person for the purpose of making his chosen ones do what he want them to do. I was evicted and it was a horrendous experience to go from paying $200 per month to $1.150. Since its inception, God has miraculously opened doors and worked many miracles for me. I have never been late with my rent and it has been just as easy to pay $1,150 as it was to pay $200 per month. I don't know how, but it's just God. And my income is even $1,200 less than it was then, God is wonderful and there is none like him. About 3 months after my eviction. I heard God say these words to me; "the reason I allowed you to lose your section 8 was to cut out all occasions to lie" he made a complete statement. I understood and knew exactly what he was talking about. My children always give me money for my birthday, mother's day and Christmas. When the housing authority agents would ask me did anybody give me money that year, I would say no! If I said yes they would take it from me by making me pay higher amounts of rent... But God was not pleased with me. God said a liar won't tarry in his sight. (Psalms 101:7-8, Rev.21:8)) Which means you will surely die. God is not the God of the dead but the living. (Matt.22:32) he also said, all liar shall have their part in the lake that burns with fire and brimstone. Lying will certainly cause you to die because lying is a sin and death is the payment for sin. After God told me that it was him who allowed me to lose my section 8 program, I am very careful now what I say so that I will not lie. I want to live. In order to live you have to please God in all your ways. Many will die because they tell lies. The scripture said to speak the truth and lie not, swear to your own hurt and change not, even if it cause you to lose everything that you have, just tell the truth and leave it to God. (Eph.4:25)(Zec.8:16). God has made a way for you to overcome death. God can not lie, it is impossible to overcome death and live if you are preparing to die for any reason, naturally or financially. You have to totally believe what Jesus said, you can't say just in case I am wrong, I'll go ahead buy some life insurance for the sake of my family, that's not faith. You have to totally walk by faith and not by sight, even though it's not always easy but you have to believe. Jesus said we are over comers. Jesus said because I live you shall live also. (John 14:19) Though you be talked about and criticized by family members and friends and those who don't share your faith, but that's alright. That's why the scripture said build up your most Holy Faith by praying in the Holy Ghost. If the righteous scarcely makes it in or overcome death, where will the unbeliever appear?

JESUS NEVER TOLD THE CHURCH TO DIE

If you will notice Jesus teaching, you will see that he never told the church to prepare to die or repent so when you die you will go to heaven. Jesus said except you repent you will likewise die:(Luke 13:3-5) what Jesus is saying, if you will repent you will not die.(when you die is the doctrine of men) to live was the good news Jesus came preaching. Jesus died in your place so you won't have to die. Jesus died and was put in a grave. That was the kind of death that he died to save you from dying. It doesn't matter how they try to fix it. Jesus didn't die a spiritual death. Your debt for death have been paid, Jesus have already paid it for you. All you have to do is repent and believe what he did for you and keep his sayings and live. You have no condemnation once you have repented and walking in the ways of the Lord. Jesus took away all your sins. The scriptures said let not sin dwell in your mortal body. (Roman6:12) If you have repented of your sins: and are living in righteousness. (Which mean, living in faith), why should you die? Jesus died that you might live, what is your purpose for dying? When you allow unbelief, which is sin, to dwell in you, you will surely die, because sin brings about death and death is of the devil, same as sickness and disease: death has been recognized as an enemy and a curse. (1 Co.15:26) even the scripture call death an enemy: <u>death is the last enemy that shall be destroyed;</u> while you are alive you will put death under your feet. When you overcome death, you will have overcome your last enemy, you will have total victory over death. Most people say everybody sins: that's no excuse, it's your responsibility <u>not to sin, (which means not to have unbelief in you)</u> because the wages of sin is death and you will give account of your sins by dying, (1 John 3:9). Whosoever is born of God does not commit sin. For because his seed remains in him and he cannot sin, because he is born of God. (1 John3:9) The seed of faith remain in you. <u>Unbelief is sin.</u> As long as the seed of faith remain in you, there is no sin in you and you are not going to do things that are ungodly nor will you do things that are of the devil. That's why you need to seek God for an understanding of how to do that, it's your responsibility to know how not to sin. You are inexcusable.

DEATH HAS REMAINED

ecause of the doctrine of men the covenant of death has remained over the church. I believe the reason the church does not preach life is because they think death is the only way to get them to heaven. I never saw in the bible where God said anybody was going to heaven. There is a way that seemed right unto a man but the end thereof; are the way of death. (Proverbs 14:12), in the end of the way that seem right to you, you die. God said that he is not willing that anybody should perish but that all should come to repentance; (2 Peter 3:9). Repentance must be a powerful thing, if a man can repent and live: repentance is a broken heart and a contrite spirit.

The only death that the scripture tell us to die is, die to your sins or to die to your unbelief. He said reckon yourselves to be dead to sin; (Romans 6:11).And as it is appointed unto men once to die, but after this the judgment, (Hebrew 9:27) if you will notice the 27th verse ends with a colon, which mean that the 28th verse should throw some light or explain the 27th verse, but it says nothing pertaining to that verse. That let you know that the next verse and also many scriptures pertaining to eternal life have been removed out of the bible. I believe the 28th verse should have read something on this order: Jesus took the appointment in the place of the believers, by dying on the cross, therefore the believers should reckon themselves to be dead, buried and risen with Christ and alive for ever more. Jesus said because I live you can also live. There is an old song that we use to sing. If I die now to my sins I won't have to die no more. God showed me many scriptures that have been removed out of the bible. They appeared in the bible about the period of a week, I read them several time and there were many of them, I marveled at them that there were so many scriptures about the knowledge of God and eternal life and seeking to know God. When I got ready to record them, they could not be found,

Blessed and holy is he that hath part in the first resurrection: on such the second death hath no power, (Rev.20:6) It's only once that is appointed unto a man to die. It is either die to your sins now or die the death that takes you to the graveyard. There shouldn't be any graveyard kind of death for you if you have repented and died to your sins; because the wages of sin is death. The scripture said to reckon yourself to be dead and buried with Christ and risen and alive for evermore. The scripture that I believe the church gets hung up on is where it said; it is appointed unto men once to die. (Heb.9:27) they fail to look at the scriptures that says die to your sins, if you die to your sins, that's once.

You are forever learning and never able to come to the knowledge of the truth, (2Tim 3:7) Jesus died once for all who believes and keep his sayings, Jesus died in your place; the scripture said: Having the form of Godliness but denying the power thereof, (2 Tim.3:5) You are denying the power of God, when you don't believe that God has the power to do what he promised to do? If you do your part GOD will do what he promised. Doing your part is to keep his sayings and believe that he died that you might live.

PREACHING LIFE
PROMOTES HEALING

I had a ministry at a convalescent home in 1998. I didn't preach death I preached life. I told the patients that Jesus died that they might live. I just said what Jesus said, soon the nurses began to tell me that since I had been ministering there, many of the patients are getting better and going home. These people are already placed in there most likely to die. Most of them are put there with not much hope of ever getting better and going home. What they need is a little hope of life. By preaching what Jesus said gave them hope. You can help others to live even longer by saying what Jesus said. There is a difference in what Jesus said and what man is saying. If what man is preaching does not line up with what Jesus came preaching then man is not preaching the gospel of Jesus Christ; he is preaching his own gospel which does not attain unto life. For I am not ashamed of the Gospel of Christ: (Romans1:16). Man is ashamed of the gospel of Jesus Christ because they don't preach from those scriptures at all, such scriptures as, if you keep my sayings you shall never die or Jesus died that we might live, when you talk on those scriptures the church will say you have left the faith, and they will not fellow-ship with you because you are using those scriptures, that they do not hear preached on. I am a living witness.

Jesus being the second Adams came to take death off the church, therefore life should be everlasting for the believers, but it's not, because they are still living in unbelief, they are dying and going through the same thing as it went through when they were under the law. They are dying and preparing men to die and that should not be. They are quick to tell you, "oh no, we don't die we just go to sleep" there is no life or mortality or immortality in the grave. Our Lord and Savior Jesus Christ: who have abolished death and has brought life and immortality to light through the Gospel (2 Timothy 1:10). It was not Paul's gospel, not Peter's gospel and not my gospel or your gospel, but the gospel of Jesus Christ.

THE DOCTRINE OF MEN

The churches believe and teaches that in order to get to Heaven you have to die, that is the doctrine of men, and it is a false doctrine, because Jesus never talked about dying and going to heaven. He never promised you heaven in the first place. Jesus promised the Kingdom, he said the kingdom of God is at hand. Seek ye first the kingdom of God and his righteousness, (his faith) and all these things will be added unto you. (Matt.6:33). When the children of Israel disobeyed the commandments of Moses teaching they were sick and dying. Jesus teaches us to repent and ye shall live, when the children of Israel obeyed the commandments, there was not a sick person among them (Exodus 15:26) as long as they walked according to the Law of that time, there was no sickness or disease among them. I believe when the church began to preach the full gospel of Jesus Christ which is life and stop preparing the church to die. And start teaching them to repent and live, they will live. And there will not be sickness and diseases in the church. There are more sickness and diseases among church people than any other people. If you ask anybody who has sickness or disease in his or her body, do they know the Lord, most of them will say, "Oh yes! I know him! It's the spiritual food of death they are being fed in the churches and unbelief that are making them sick and causing them to die.

If the church has the kind of power that it has preaching partial of the gospel of Jesus Christ, just think what great power it would have if it preached the complete full gospel, when I speak of power I am speaking of knowledge and of the anointing power of the Holy Ghost. When the church start preaching and teaching the scriptures that they never talk about; it will have the kind of power that it had in the Apostle Paul's days. The devil won't be able to stand in your mist. People won't be coming in and shooting up the church and doing all kind of ungodly things. The church has lost its power you might as well face it. Verily, Verily I say unto you. If a man keep my saying, (my prophecies) he shall never see death. (John 8:51). Jesus died that we may live. It's time to start preaching the truth to God's people. Jesus said his words are spirit and they are truth. His words are anointed and It is the anointing that destroys the yoke. But as many as received him to them gave he the power to become the sons of God, even to them who believe on his name. (John 1:12) The more knowledge of God the church receive the more power it will have and the more anointing the church will have.

Even if you just believe on the name of the son of God, you have the power to become a son of God. That is so powerful. But not every church preach sonship less knowing accepting son-ship God has giving you the power to become a son of God, if you have received him or even believed on his name, you have power to become a son of God. But you have to believe and accept it. The bible said, believe it in your heart and confess it with your mouth and you can have what you say. To become a son of God, you don't have to attend a bible college, you don't have to set in a class for six weeks, and you don't have to have hands laid on you to become a son of God. You just believe it and receive it. When I received my sonship I said something like this; I believe it in my heart and I confess it with my mouth that God has given me the power to become a son of God, so therefore I am a son of God. When I made that confession; suddenly I felt something move in my stomach like a baby. At that moment I heard the Holy Spirit say, Christ is now birth in you. You might not have that same experience that I had, but if you believe it in your heart and confess it with your mouth by saying that you are a son of God. You will suddenly become a son of God, no doubt about. Jesus said: "except you repent you will also perish."(Luke 13:3-5) death is a curse, so why would the true and living God take you from under the curse of death by giving his only begotten son to die for you and then put you right back under the curse of death? Jesus died that you might live," He said repent and ye shall live) I believe the church have a choice to live or die. God said "I set before you this day life and death, he said choose life" (Deut.30:19). That let you know you have a choice. The only choice a sinner have, is to repent or not repent, and when he repent he is no more a sinner, I'll never understand why the church teaches to repent and then say, so you when you die you will go to heaven, Jesus said repent that you might live.

THE PLAGUES ARE SICKNESS, DISEASE AND DEATH

When the church began to say what Jesus said there won't be so much sickness and diseases in the churches and so many of our children wouldn't be born sickly... Jesus said, "if any man add to the prophecy of this book God shall add unto him the plaques, that are written in this book and "if a man take away from the prophecy of this book, God will take his name out of the book of life,(Rev 22:18-19) the prophecy are the sayings of Jesus. "He that overcomes death shall inherit all things. (Rev.21:7) God never said we shall inherit heaven, he said we shall inherit all things. (Hebrew 11:5) Enoch overcame death and was translated without dying and so was Elisha they didn't go the way of the grave, they didn't die they were each translated. God is the same today as he was yesterday and forever. (Heb.13:8) God never changes, but if we don't change we will surely die. We are transformed (changed) by the renewing of our mind, the renewing of our mind come by the knowledge of God. Paul said that we shall be changed from this mortal to immortality. (1 Cor. 15: 51-52). If that's the case, the only time you are mortal is right now while you live in your physical body. If you die you are no longer mortal and will never be mortal again. If you die that would be call corruption. Nevertheless death reigned from Adam to Moses. (Rom.5:14) Moses was a (type of Christ) when Jesus came, he brought in a more perfect way. "For if ye live after the flesh ye shall die, but if ye through the spirit do mortify the deeds of the (flesh) ye shall live. (Rom 8:13)

GETTING A RIGHTEOUS MAN TO THE KINGDOM

The scripture let us know that after you repent you have to be separated and keep yourselves clean and unspotted from the world so you can be changed from this mortal to total spirit. Jesus said that he died that you might live. The church has kept you under the banner of death, by its teachings. Jesus said, "If you keep my sayings you will never see death"—in other word he said if you keep my prophecy or say what I say you will never die. I have not seen where Jesus changed anything that he said, so therefore you can't change anything that he said. The church try's to justify preaching death by saying what they think Paul was saying. When he said for to me, it is better for me to die and be with the Lord, for to live is Christ and to die is gain. (Phil.1:21) If you will notice—Paul did not say it is better for us to die and be with the Lord, or it is better for the church to die and be with the Lord. He said it is better for me (for himself) it is better to die and be with the Lord, he didn't say if we live is Christ, he said "if I live is Christ and if I die is gain," Paul was speaking only for himself and about himself. He knew the suffering that should befall him. Jesus told him the thing that was going to happen to him. Paul was saying if I live everything that Jesus told me that's going to happen to me, is true: (that is Christ!). But if I die I don't have to go through all that suffering, that Jesus told me that's going to happen to me (that is gain!) that would have been like beating the system, but Paul had to go through it for the sake of the gospel and for the sake of those who would receive the gospel. Paul said, "I was born for this purpose" Paul did not pronounce death on the church neither did Jesus pronounce death on the church. Jesus died that the church might live. Jesus said he didn't come to condemn the world but that the world might be saved, (might live) condemn mean death. When a perpetrator goes to trail and they say that he is condemned, their plan is to kill that perpetrator. Paul said: "whether we live or die we are the Lord's, (Rom.14:8). So why not preach the truth and say it like Jesus said it and live and leave how you are going to get out of your physical body to God, because it is his business and he know how to get you where he want you, so let God be true and live.

REPENT AND LIVE

Jesus gave his disciples power and the authority over all devils and to cure diseases and he sent them to preach the Kingdom of God and to heal the sick, (Luke 9:1-2), These signs shall follow them that believe, if you can believe and receive those scriptures why can't you believe and use the same scriptures where Jesus say unless you repent you will die, instead of saying repent and get ready to die. There has to be some reason why we never hear preachers use those scriptures, where Jesus said, except you repent you will likewise perish; even if they do say them they don't seem to understand what the word perish mean. Why they don't know that perish mean death? That's why God said my people perish for the lack of knowledge. If you keep my sayings you will never see death (John 8:51) Jesus said, that he died that you might live, you never hear that preached in a message. Jesus can't make a mistake and all of his words are true and they are life. Just use his words and leave it to God, that's his business, and that's how we walk by faith by trusting what Jesus say, and believing that his words are true.

Jesus said that there are some standing here, which shall not taste of death till they see the Son of man coming in his Kingdom. Jesus was talking to the Pharisees and the Sadducees who came and was tempting him and wanting him to show them a sign, Jesus told them that there will be no sign except the sign of Jonah,(Matt.16:1-28). we know that Jonah was disobedient to God we know what happened to him: the apostles was looking forward to the coming of the kingdom of God and their prayers was let thy kingdom come, I believe his kingdom has already come, because he said that the kingdom of God is at hand, and also the kingdom of God is within you, he knew that some who were present there that day would keep his saying, because they believed on him and would still be alive when his kingdom come and would enter into his kingdom. Jesus said I go away to prepare a place for you; he was talking to the believers who kept his saying. I will come again and receive you unto myself, he will receive you into his kingdom, he knew there were others there beside believers who did not say or practice nor believe what he was saying or what he was teaching and somebody would not keep his saying, because they didn't believe in him nor did they believe his sayings.

"For God so loved the world that he gave his only begotten Son, that whosoever believeth in him (should) not perish but should have everlasting life. (John 3:15) That scripture didn't say (shall) not perish," it said should not perish. I noticed how that scripture read in my early twenties and also the scripture that said, we have a choice to live or die: where God said I set before you this day, life and death; he said to choose life, there are so much in God's word that people just pass right over without noticing, as a young woman many times I wonder in my heart about John 3:16, why it said "whosoever believe on him (should not perish (die) instead of saying shall not perish) and why the preachers and teachers would always say, shall not perish instead of saying should not perish, and why nobody ever said anything about how that scripture was read. The scripture said we (should) not perish and yet everybody is dying. It said for God so loved the world, that he gave his only begotten Son, which is (Jesus) that whosoever believeth in him should not die (and yet they die). There is a different in (should not and shall not) so if you believe in him, you should live. There is a reason why the people die and that's because of the spiritual food they are being fed, and their dying is in vain. It does not profit anything for themselves or anybody else to die: neither does God get any pleasure out of there dying. He said for I have no pleasure in the death of him that die therefore turn yourself and live. (Ezekiel 18:32)

UNBELIEF MUST BE
BURNED OUT

God does not throw his people away because they die, although he said it's not his will that any should perish. For the Lord is good; and his mercy is ever lasting and his truth endured to all generation,(Psalms100:5) I believe if a confessed believer die he or she will have to go through the fire to burn out the unbelief that caused them to die. I'm not talking about a lake of fire but about the truth of God's word. God word is a consuming fire. You will hear the truth that you don't want to hear now, over and over. You will have to be made perfect; the believers who died cannot be made perfect except (we who have the ministry of reconciliation) make them perfect. (Heb.11:40). The Holy Spirit instructed me how to make my son perfect after he had been dead for three months. If a believer who have confessed that Jesus Christ is the son of God die: they died without receiving the promise of God, which is eternal life. Because of the teaching and indoctrination of death that they received or for the lack of knowledge or they died because they were not taught to keep Jesus saying, neither were they taught to seek for the knowledge of God. If you don't believe or keep Jesus sayings now while you live, you won't believe or keep them after you die. I *heard* Pastor Harlo White say in one of his message that "you can't die with unbelief in you and all of a sudden you believe after you die" it doesn't work like that. There can't be any unbelief in you in the present of God and his Holy angels. If you don't believe the message of Jesus Christ, you are damned already. I believe if you will keep his saying you will not die, words are so powerful; even your own words are powerful, therefore you must know how powerful Gods word are. For the word of God is quick and powerful, and sharper, than any two edged sword, piercing even to the dividing asunder of soul and spirit; and of the joints and morrow of the bone and is a discerner of the thoughts and intents of the heart. (Heb. 4:12). You cannot be saved from death if you don't believe God's word. When you ask why people are still dying, it's because they don't believe neither do they keep his sayings.

THE DEVIL SAID I WAS
GOING TO DIE

When I first received the Baptism of the Holy Ghost at eighteen years old, the next day all day long the devil told me that I was going to die because I had receive the Holy Ghost. My stomach got so sore I could hardly walk. That evening I told my father that all day long something told me that I was going to die. We were taught that God was the one who made you die. I didn't know it was the devil talking to me, but when I told my father that because I had received the Holy Ghost something told me that I was going to die. My father said, baby you just got ready to live. The minute he said that, instantly all the soreness left my stomach, I know that was the Holy Spirit speaking through my father. My father was a firm believer and teacher of saying you have to get saved so when you die you'll go to heaven. But that day he said because I had received the Holy Ghost that I just got ready to live. If my father had followed the church teaching and said, well baby you are saved now, you are ready to die. I probably would have died, but he said baby you just got ready to live. Life is what gives eternal life; death does not give you eternal life. The devil come to steal, kill and destroy, but Jesus came to give life. Get saved so you'll be ready to die is what my dad always taught, because that's what he was taught and that's what the church is still teaching. **"get saved or I will give you the right hand of fellowship or come and join the church so when you die you will go to heaven"**. That's the false teaching and doctrine of men and that's the way I was taught and I believed it, until God reveal the truth to me. I was blinded to the truth as many are today, but God opened the eyes of my understanding.

Most people never know to search the scripture to see how Jesus said things. Jesus said except you repent you will die. If people would read the scriptures and believed what Jesus said, death wouldn't be a common thing in the churches. We were taught not to question what the pastor say. I believe that you should sometimes question what you are being taught. If you believe it's different than what the scripture says. You should always believe what Jesus says over and above of what any man say. I believe if you did, the church and you and your children would have more abundant life and death would be a rare thing in the church. In the days of the apostles, death was not a common thing in the church. Church people are sickly and dying for the lack of knowledge or unbelief. They are being programed to die by death indoctrination. By saying repent and get saved so when you die you will go to heaven, death is a debt that people pay for the sins that they claimed to be saved from. Then they will say Jesus has already paid that debt by dying. Why are you still trying to pay it again by dying?

HAS BEEN DEATH
INDOCTRINATED

We have all been death indoctrinated by the church. In 1994 God told me to come out of the church. I was astonished and terrified that God would tell me or anybody to come out of the church. The church was all I knew and it took me about four years to come out. Finally God told me in no uncertain tone to come out of the church and he told me why. He said I can't continue to hear the preachers preach the message of death and the Holy Spirit preach Life and obtain unto life" I didn't know that God would ever tell anybody to come out of the church. I always believed that you had to go to church in order to be saved and I always found comfort in the church. God have not told me to tell anybody else to come out of the church. God told me to come out from among them and be separated. If God had not told me why he told me to come out of the church and if I had not remembered all the other unusual things that God had been showing me or speaking to me, I don't know if I could have ever been able to believe that was God telling me to come out of the Church. I think I would have thought it was the devil talking to me. I was taught that it was a sin not to go to church. Church was all I knew. I received many blessings in the church. For me to obey and fulfill God's purpose for me I had to come out. I was scared and I was ashamed to tell anybody that I don't go to church. I was afraid to come out because of what the people would say. I knew they would say that I had left the faith and that worried me it didn't matter what God was saying, it bothered me. I was in a very tough situation it was not a walk in the park for me. I was more afraid to disobey God then I was to come out of the church. I thought I was the only one in this faith beside Brother Karl Stokes, the messenger that God sent to me. I was thinking, oh God this is so hard nobody believe what I say not even my own children. I became angry with the preacher for teaching us the things that they had taught us until God said to me, it's not their fault. That's what they were also taught. He said not all of them know the truth, he said but some do know the truth. Some would rather have the biggest church then to preach the truth. In my spirit I was wrestling with it, that's why it took me so long to come out. Even today I still have to remember and remind myself of the things God told me and why he told me to come out of the church. Every time God told me to come out I would say to myself no he didn't say that he said such and such. I knew what he was saying but I didn't understand why, until he said that I couldn't continue to hear the preachers preach the message of death and the Holy Spirit preach life and attain unto life. That's when I really understood why I had to come out of church. But I was still scared of what the church people would say. The last time he told me to come out, he said it like he really meant it and I knew he meant business. God's voice made me feel so fearful and I knew I had better obey this time. I obeyed no matter what the people said and they said plenty. I felt so lonely. I had nobody to communicate with without getting into an augment or disputes. Finally I found fellowship with a ministry of like faith. God has blessed me to have fellowship by audio tapes and CD'S with a great ministry in Chicago, IL. God told me to plant seed in that great ministry to support it. The Harlo White Ministries-Out-Reach Church of Chicago, IL., Pastor Harlo White is a man whom God has let down in the deep of his word. I have greatly been inspired and blessed. He also has a radio ministry in Chicago, IL Before God began to reveal the mysteries of God to me: two or three times per year in tears, the Holy Spirit would constrain me say; "Lord let me down in the deep secrets of your word". God began to reveal his Knowledge and his mysteries to me.

GOD KNOW HOW TO GET
YOU WHERE HE WANT

The first time God told me to come out of the church was when I saw the Jurisdictional Bishop do something so abusive to the woman who was his State Supervisor of Women, right in the presence of about fifty or sixty Superintendents and Elders. He put his finger on her nose and said you better get yourself together, I said, "Oh my God, I have got to get out of here. I didn't know that God was working in order to get me out of the church. It didn't matter as much to me of how abusive they were to me I accepted it. I would never have left the church and God knew that. God know what it takes to move you to do what he want you to do. I thought it was just me leaving the church on my own, because of what I saw happen to the State Supervisor. I didn't know that was God's way of getting me out of the church. A few months later I was invited to a church in Ventura, California; as I was getting dressed to go, I heard a voice saying to me, "I didn't bring you out of that church for you to go back into another church. I knew it was God, and it scared me.

Immediately I said no! He didn't say that, he said for me not to tie myself up in church because I am an evangelist I have to go from church to church to carry this message. Fear will make you lie. All alone I knew that was not what he said but I was scared and in shock! I had never heard such thing as God telling anybody to come out of the church, I could not believe he was actually telling me to come out of the church, I loved the church. I kept going. I hadn't had any other life but church life. I had been in church all of my life and loved it. Instead of coming out I united with another church and seem to have moved straight to the top for the first time in my life in the Evangelist Department. I thought I was on my way to travel and do revivals as I always wanted to do. I seem to have found favors that I never had in church before. I was EVANGELIST ZELMA'MONEY! Two years later the pastor put me out of that church. He told me he didn't want me there, I was really hurt, I asked him why? "The pastor told me that I go too much," "I said, no pastor, I'm here every Sunday" and that was the truth. I was there every Sunday. Then he said you don't give any money. I said I'm on a fixed low income. I said; I pay my tithes and gave offering when I can, and I also try to pay other dues. I left. I told myself that this happened because I had tied myself up in church and God was punishing me for not going out on the evangelist field to do revivals. Although nobody had asked me to do a revival but I thought that was why God was allowing this to happen to me. I had never heard of anybody ever being put out of the **Church of God In Christ**, not even when they were doing bad and wrong things. I knew I was not doing anything wrong. This was my first time ever seeing that happen and have never heard of anything like that happening since. Little did I know that was Gods way of getting me out of the church and that's what it took and more. I had been mistreated many times in the church, but nothing could drive me away. Many times I had been appointed to be the main speaker and without anybody telling me that they were putting somebody else up to speak. I was not told. However my name would be on the program as speaker, but nobody would do me the common (courtesy) of letting me know that I was not bringing the message. Most of the times the Holy Spirit, would say you are not going to bring the message. That would give me time to compose myself. It was a hurting thing and so embarrassing but I said nothing and I did nothing. It took God to let me see somebody else being abused to get me out of there. Things like that happened to me personally and being abused went on for years and years yet I did nothing and I said nothing. I thought that was just my cross that I had to bare. Getting hurt so many times was not the reason I came out of the church. If that had been the case I never would have come out of the church. I loved church. God's purpose for me was to come out because of the preaching of the message of death. God want me to attain unto life. That's why I had to come out. The Holy Spirit preaches life and that's what

Jesus preached was life because he is life. The church has been death indoctrinated and that's why I am writing this book to share this truth with as many who will accept it. Everyone who has this message must also share it, to try to save Gods people from death.

GETTING MY DIRECTION

After my pastor put me out of the church I decided to go to my friend and her husband's church. She and I had been friends since our early twenties, long before they got married. That Sunday I walked in the church a little late, he had just got up to bring the message and when I walked in: he looked at me and said I was going to preach on such and such but I am going to change my message. I am going to preach about people who make God sick. I said to myself, oh my God! now we have a sick God on hand, he preached about people who leave one church and go to another one, he had already tried to make me go back to the church that God had told me that he didn't bring me out of for me to back into another church, I knew I couldn't go back there, because God had said that he brought me out. That was the church where the Bishop put his finger on the State Supervisors nose and said you better get yourself together. Now I decided I can't go to my friend church either. I said I'll just go to the largest Church Of God In Christ in Los Angeles and get loss in the crowd until God gives me my directions. So I did, not knowing that God was leading me all the time. That was in 1994, I went through all their new member classes and I was glad to do it. I became a member in about 6 weeks, my membership number was 2752. I was invited to work in the Evangelist department. You have to use your title there and in most of the churches so they will know how much money to make you pay. Oh yes that's the way its set up in the churches. You are forever paying for a title and they don't come cheap. For every event you pay, but we didn't mind paying because that meant when your name is called you are not embarrassed. Believe me your name is going to be called if you have a title. I stayed there for about a year or more until I got my directions from God. I wrote the pastor a letter and thanked him for allowing me to worship with his congregation while waiting for God to give me my directions, now that I have them, I'll be moving on. I never heard from him but I know that he got my letter. I got no more letters from the evangelist department telling me how much money they wanted from me for different occasions. If my name had not been on their list they wouldn't have known I was there. I know the pastor didn't know I was there. He may have seen me are read my name on something concerning money but he couldn't have put the name and face together as he could many of the others members because the church was so huge. I enjoyed the time that I was there. When it came to Leaders he was one of the best.

BE MADE PERFECT

God want us to be made perfect, the second time God told me to come out of the church was with a scripture and that was the first time that I had ever understood what this scripture meant, Therefore leaving the principles of the doctrine of Christ, let us go on to perfection. (Heb. 6:1) Instantly I understood it, I said ooh, that's what that scripture mean, Christ is the church, God is telling me to leave the principles of the doctrine of the church so I can go on to perfection, then I heard the Holy Spirit say, "the church can't make you perfect the pastor can't make you perfect, only the Holy Spirit can make you perfect. The principles of the doctrine of the church that Paul was talking about leaving: is the death doctrine of preparing people to die. It's not God's will that any should perish: I was beginning to understand what God was trying to do in my life. Be ye therefore perfect, even as your Father which is in Heaven is perfect: (Matt 5:48) God want us to be perfect and live, I have heard preachers all my life say ooh, God know we can't be perfect. I have never heard one say—God I know that you said for us to be perfect, but I don't know how to do that, Lord, show me or show us how to be perfect. When you do that, then you are beginning to seek for the knowledge of God. You seek for the knowledge of God by asking him to reveal himself to you or reveal something to you. You need to realize what the scripture mean when it say if any man think he know anything, he don't know nothing as he ought to know" I remember when the Holy Spirit would move upon me about two or three times per year and I would say Lord let me down in the deep secrets of your word and I would be crying when I said it. Finally I begin to say that I must be crazy. What are the deep secrets of his word? Why do I cry when I say that? I was seeking to know God without knowing it. I was never taught to seek to know God. I was like everybody else. I thought I already knew him. Only God can reveal himself to you and that will come by you seeking to know him. All through the bible Old and the New Testament God tells us to seek to know him. Each scripture said something pertaining to Eternal Life.

When you began to seek to know God, he will begin to reveal himself to you, we have heard of him, we have read about him, but we don't know him until he reveals himself to us. The more you seek to know him the more he reveals himself to you and the more like him you will become, and also the more perfect you will become. God said seek to know me. You are transformed by the renewing of your mind. (Romans12:2) The more revelation knowledge you get of him, the more your mind is renewed and the more you are transformed into who he is or the more like him you become. We feel his love, we receive his blessings and his healings, but only God can reveal himself to you. We think we know him when we get born again, but we don't know him no more than a new birth baby know his mother, as he grow older he will know more about her. As we follow on to know God we will receive more knowledge of him through revelations.

GOD WANT HIS PEOPLE
TO SEEK TO KNOW HIM

About four years ago God gave me prophetic revelation statement. He said my people don't know me. They know about me because of what they ask me for and what I do for them but they don't know me. I could hear God in the spirit mocking them how they sound when they say certain things. "I know God, because I ask Him for a car, and he gave m e" a car. I ask him for a house and he gave "m e e" a house. He said, they don't know me; when they began to seek to know me. Then I will begin to reveal to them mysteries, even the mystery, "which have been hidden from ages to ages and from generations to generations that I am manifesting to my saints today. (Col. 1:26) He said, "That will be all about me. People think because they accepted him as their personal savior they know him. When you accept a study in college to be a doctor you don't know how to practice being a doctor just because you accepted the study. You might be given all kind of helps even a scholarship. But in order to be a doctor you have to seek for that knowledge. That's the same thing with God the only different is you seek God for the knowledge of him by faith, asking him to reveal himself to you. Man might try to break that word down to you where you can understand it by telling you all he have learned by reading or studying. But if he didn't seek God for the knowledge of God most likely he don't have the knowledge of God and he might not know any more then you know; the scripture said if any man think that he know anything, he know nothing as he ought to know.

OBEDIENT TO GOD

I understand what Paul meant, when he said, fail not to assemble yourselves together as some have, that's true. As long as you are assembling yourself together with those whom God want you to assemble yourselves together with. You wouldn't assemble yourself together very well with people who don't agree with what God who is the Holy Spirit has revealed to you and commissioned you to do, that would be a lot of confusion. So you just obey God and let them do what they believe what they are doing is right, maybe that's what God want them to do if not maybe God will let them know. When God told me the second time to come out of the church I knew what God was saying to me but it was so hard. I had never been out of the church before. I know that His grace and mercy was with me because it's dangerous to disobey God at any time. When I heard Gods voice in no uncertain tone, a great fear came over me, I know without God's mercy, you don't get to disobey Him and come out alright. It doesn't matter who don't believe what you say, you are responsible to God for your own self. He told me to come out from among them

109

and be separated said the Lord. I knew I was in trouble if I failed to obey the voice of the Lord. God was so merciful to me. He had allowed me about four years to disobey Him. Even after about half of that time I knew it was him. I was thinking maybe it will go away and I won't have to come out of the church. Actually I was ashamed of the gospel that Jesus preached because nobody else that I ever known was preaching it. Many of you are saying you are not ashamed, but evidently you are because you are not preaching Jesus Gospel. The gospel that you are preaching is not the full gospel of Jesus Christ if it was, you would preach those scriptures that you never talk about. Scriptures like, (St. John, 8:51). Maybe you are like I was I didn't want to be different from the other people in the church. It was scary I knew people would act differently toward me, yet I didn't have a clue of how differently they would act toward me. I believe my own child almost said that I should be dead to be teaching what I said God had revealed to me and I know my child love me, I don't know what all God has revealed to him but he is just as much into the knowledge of God as I am. He always pray and thank God for me and for the knowledge that he has revealed to me.

I was speaking at a church and I said that Jesus died that we might live and never die. Because of fear some people jumped up and ran out of the church. Nobody wants to die, but for fear of what they had never heard preached and had not been taught they ran. Jesus said the fearful and unbelievers shall have their part in the lake

that burns with fire and brimstone. Jesus said he died that we might live.

We were taught that everybody had to die in order to go to heaven. Jesus said that he came to redeem us from death. Even the smartest theologian who went to bible college and have their doctorate degrees, don't seem to know or understand the importance of (redeem from death). It means that you don't have to die, even though you were born in sin and death. Jesus bought you back with his own blood. That's how God has made a way for the believers to come out of that death that you were born in and live. Jesus came to redeem you from sin and death. Jesus Know it's not your fault what you were taught. For the lack of knowledge, what you were taught is killing you. Theologians have to seek to know God in order to have the knowledge of God. He said the day you hear my voice, harden not your heart. Some people put scriptures together to make them come close to saying what they want to believe or what they have been taught to believe. Nobody told me about the scriptures to read about Jesus sayings, as I am trying to tell you in this book. Jesus said that my way is so plain, which mean his word is so plain that a fool can't error. You don't have to run references from scripture to scripture to understand what Jesus is saying. His sayings are plain because he said exactly what he meant. The scripture said; he that has an ear to hear let him, hear what the Spirit has to say to the church. His word is Spirit and truth.

CHOSEN BY GOD

I was born for this purpose to declare the truth concerning the preaching of the gospel of Jesus Christ that we might live and not die. That was the good news that Jesus came preaching that he died that we might live. As I was being born God told my father that this child is chosen. My father preached that over the pulpit all of his life that he had one daughter that he know is chosen of God and he would say he believe that he have another daughter that is chosen of God though God didn't tell him that. There were eight girls and four boys born to my mom and dad. My dad said about 10:00 PM the night that my mom was in labor with me, God told him that the child will be born at 2:00 o'clock in the morning and he told my mom that he was going to get some rest because the baby won't be born until 2:00 o'clock, he said, that my mom looked at him with amazement. My father said as a big town clock in Tyler, TX struck 2:00 o'clock I was making my arrival into this world.

This book that I am writing God told me to write it. He told me verbally to write a book. It was for the same purpose that God told the prophet Ezekiel to warn the people and if they repent they will surely live but if he failed to warn the people and they die and their blood will be required at his hands, (Ezekiel 3:18).I began to tell the people in the church, that God has revealed to me Eternal Life, without dying. Sometimes people would jump up and run out of the church because of fear and unbelief. The scripture said the fearful and the unbelievers shall have their part in the lake that burns with fire and brimstone, (Rev.21:8) my own sister and some others said to me, "show me somebody who have lived forever and I will believe you" that really disturbed me. That night I said to God! "God I need something from you, there are people who want me to show them somebody who have lived for ever", and when I said that, straightaway, I heard God say; "Show them yourself! I chose you in me before the foundation of the world and you are still alive" I was astounded to hear God say that. I was not expecting God to say show them yourself. Though I knew that I was chosen of God and that answer really appeased me. Every believer is not chosen of God, many are called but few are chosen. I was talking to somebody about two weeks ago, the later part of June 2010 of how fast the time is passing. The Holy Spirit said" I said except I shorten the days" after that I looked up the scripture in the bible; except those days should be shortened, there should no flesh be saved: but for the elect's sake those days shall be shortened. (Matthews 24:22) God want your flesh to be saved, he don't want you to die. God made known to me that because of the days being shortened, a year is no more than six months. Time is winding up, whatever you do, do it quickly and as unto the Lord and in all your ways acknowledge God.

I married at a very young age of fifteen years old and yes I was a virgin when I got married. I got pregnant with my first child two months after I got married. My father had me to sit down so he could talk to me, and he said, now is the time that you shape your child's life. "You should always try to have a kind and sweet spirit and always do the right thing for the sake of your unborn child" my father was a man of wisdom, he taught us to do the right things as much he knew how. As a child if we did anything bad I believed that God would reveal it to my dad. At that time I would rather have had the wrath of God then the wrath of my father. I believe I would have remained a virgin even if my father had said I could not get married. I was mostly always an obedient child. Parent in that day had the old fashion idea, that if your daughter want to get married you had better let her, because if you don't she would bring an open shame on you and on your ministry. I really wasn't anxious to get married, but my father didn't say no that I couldn't get married. If dad had said no I couldn't get married and had told me not to see that man any more. I would have obeyed. As girls called it back in that day when a man ask her for sex, she would say he asked me an unfair question and that is what was happening, he was asking me unfair questions and I was afraid to do what he wanted because I knew God would reveal it to my father. That's why I got married. It was not a happy marriage at all but by the grace of God I survived.

I am writing concerning spirits: all kinds of spirits, with different operations. I am not judging anybody I'm just writing what God told me to write. God told me years ago that anything that you can't see with your naked eye is a spirit. Though you can't see it with your naked eyes, you can see what it does to a person body or to their mind. Cancer is a spirit and you can't see cancer with your naked eye but you can see what it does to a person body. All sickness and diseases are spirits and they are of the devil including death is a spirit and it is of the devil: serial killing is a spirit and these spirits makes you just what they are. There is a spirit that is controlling and messing up many young men lives, and that is masturbation. Instead of some men spending time in the bedroom with their wife, they are setting in front of the computer or TV masturbating and that spirit is getting just as big a hold on them as the homosexual spirit is getting on those who practice it: young men are getting married and their wives are in bed suffering and burning waiting for their husband to come to bed and in the meantime he prefer getting his kicks in front of the computer watching pornography movies or talking on the phone or internet to strange women who he don't even know and using his imaginations which is ruining many marriages. That spirit is just as powerful as the sodomy spirit which is homosexuality and so many are accepting and doing whatever it desires. Just like the city of Sodomy and Gomorrah, that God allowed to be destroyed, he said because of their wicked ways. so many claim to be born that way, I don't know how they were born but God called it a rebellious spirit that needed to be bind and cashed out. Like the boy in the bible who was born blind that was a spirit of blindness. And the boy who had a lunatic spirit in him, who would cast himself into the fire and sometimes in the water (Matt 17:14-21 and Mark (9:17 -29)), that spirit needed to be cast out, which would only come out by faith and prayer. Jesus casted those spirits out; my own son had a spirit that God called a rebellious spirit. God told me to bind that spirit and loose him from it so he can go on to perfection to be made perfect. Before he died, I prayed so many times that God would deliver my son from homosexuality. One day I cried out to God and said, Lord when is my son going to be delivered? This is what God's said to me. "When it finally dawned upon the slave that he was free" I had read a book about the emancipation of the slaves and how so many of them continued to stay and be slaves after they were set free. But when it finally dawned upon them that they were free and were no longer slaves. Then they began to leave to be the free men and women that God made them to be. When and if it dawn upon these men and women who have enslaved themselves to that life style of sodomy and homosexuality by fantasying themselves of the sexual pleasures that caused that spirit to grow stronger and stronger until it completely controlled them, which also comes with a rebellious spirit. It is hard to cast out a rebellious spirit: unless you want it to be cast out; it's not easy. When you think about it, nothing is easy. The same with cigarettes you have to want to stop smoking. You can be free with the help of God, if you want to be free and when it dawn upon you that God made you for one sexual purpose and that is to sexually serve the opposite sex. God said if a man lay with a man or a woman lay with a woman, he or she is worthy of death and not only that, all who have pleasure in what that man or woman is doing will receive the same judgment and that is death. Even their women did chance the natural use of a man into that which is against nature. .And likewise also the men, leaving the natural use of the woman, burned in their lust one toward another, men with men working that which is unseemly:((Roman 1: 26-32) if you are a man and you lay with another man, God said you will die and he also said you are worthy to die. (But not worthy to be murdered: but to die.) I am not condemning gay people, God love you same as he does anybody else. God said that he have no respect of person, (Rom.2:11) gay, straight, and everybody else will be judged if they continue in their way, the judgment is the same, everybody shall give an account of every deed that is done in their body. (Roman 2:6-11). Gay people have as much chance of being saved as those who are being death indoctrinated in the churches. Each will end in death if they continue: after you die you will have a chance to be made perfect same as everybody else who die, if you have confessed that Jesus Christ is the son of God. What is causing gay and straight to die is sin, what is causing the church people to die is sin of unbelief. The judgment is the same and that is death. The spirit of God spoke this in my spirit one day and said, it's not that most people who call themselves Christians who die, is worthy to die but many die for the lack of knowledge and the death indoctrination by their religious leaders that cause them to not believe in Jesus teaching of eternal life. The Holy Spirit also spoke and said to me "if it had been my purpose for a man to lay with a man or a woman to lay with a woman I would have given each of them two productive genital organs", so they could bring forth fruit (children). (Luke13:6-9) anything that can't bring forth fruit God cut it down therefore God made woman for the man, God love marriages, marriage was the first institution that God ordained and set in order and it was between a man and a women.

JESUS CHRIST IS THE SON OF GOD

I had nine children and I taught each of them that Jesus Christ is the Son of God. Also the church teaches that Jesus is the son of God. Each one of my children have confessed with their mouth and believed in their hearts that Jesus Christ is the Son of God including my son Jerome who died. Therefore according to scripture they shall be saved. Which mean that Jerome is saved from eternal damnation, God said that you and your house shall be saved. I believe every word that God say and I believe it's working for me and my children, of course they have to believe and keep Jesus sayings for themselves or they will die. Everyone has to keep Jesus sayings if they want to live. Jesus said if you take away from this prophecy (which is his sayings) you take your name out of the book of life and if you add to this prophecy, you add the plagues of this life to you, (the plagues are sickness, disease and death), Jesus said his way is straight and narrow that the righteous will scarcely make it in, if the righteous scarcely makes it in, where will the unbelievers appear. If you believe in Jesus you should believe every word that's written in his gospel and keep his sayings and live. You will have a chance of reconciliation if you die and you have believed in heart and confessed with your mouth that Jesus Christ is the Son of God. According to scripture you shall be saved.

LET BROTHERLY LOVE
CONTINTUE

The scriptures said, "Let brotherly love continue" immediately following that it said; "Be not forgetful to entertain strangers for where by some have entertained angels unawares" (Hebrew 13:1-2) we have been taught that when a man die there is nothing else you can do for that man, but the good news is, there is something you can do and I am a living witness. There is something that those who have the ministry of reconciliation can do to help those believers that died and those who had confessed that Jesus Christ is the son of God. God told me to bind that spirit that was in my son, that God called a rebellious spirit. I bind and loosed my son from that spirit so he could go on to perfection to be made perfect. This happened three months after my son died; therefore I know there is something the believer can do to let brotherly love continue. I believe we who have accepted this truth and have become sons of God and have the ministry of reconciliation can reconcile the spirits of just men back to God. God said that he gave us power to become sons of God, (St. John 1:12). As believers and sons of God we have the responsibility to minister to the spirits of the believers who die. We are ministering angels. And these all, having obtained a good report through faith, received not the <u>promise,</u> (Heb.13:39,40) Because they died,(they received not eternal life):(that's also talking about the believers of today who by faith obtain a good report but they died and the <u>promise was not death</u>, the <u>promise is eternal life)</u> God having provided some better thing for us,<u>(who are the sons of God</u>;) that those believers who died for the lack of knowledge and yet they had the faith and did all the good that they knew how to do, still had to be made perfect. The sons of God are the ones who made or will make them perfect; That scripture mean that we who have believed and kept the sayings of Jesus and those who have accepted to be a son of God, are the ones who should make perfect the spirits of the believers who die.

If you died the death, that is a natural death, you did not receive the promise which is eternal life, your spirit has to be made perfect and it cannot be made perfect except the sons of God make it perfect, the spirits of those believers who died, are groining and waiting for the manifestation of the sons of God (Romans 8:19) to deliver their spirit from the bondage of death so they can go on to the place of perfection that they might be made perfect and live in the presence of God forever,(1 Thes.4:17) Your spirit is the eternal part of you that must be resurrected and reconciled to God if you died and was a believer and had confessed that Jesus Christ is the son of God. Your spirit didn't die the eternal death. We who are alive and remain alive are the ones who will let brotherly love continue. We are the ones who will make perfect the spirits of those believers who died without the promise. They died without eternal life. We deliver them from the bondages of death that they might be made perfect. Brotherly love combined with faith and the supernatural power of God is a powerful source.

POWER TO MINISTER
TO THE STORM

God used me to minister to the storm and to hurricane Rita. I was watching the people on the freeway trying to get to safety some had died from the fumes and there had been an explosion of oxygen on a bus that killed some senior citizens. At that moment I felt so helpless and felt that I could do nothing. All of a sudden this anointing came upon me and I rose up in my spirit and said I am a son of God and that should account for something and it seemed as though I entered into the spirit realm, I was praying with the power of God with regard to what he said my calling was. God said that my calling is divination. I began to rebuke the spirit of death in the name of Jesus. I said Lord enough people have died from the storms even hurricane Katrina and I don't want another person to die from this storm, don't let anybody be killed by this storm, God I mean not even one be killed. The next day the news media Anthony Cooper on CNN kept saying over and over. "I don't understand why nobody was killed, this was a bad storm" he continued to say that over and over. He was amazed. I continue to watch Anthony Cooper as he was out reporting the storm and it was a bad storm. But God answered my prayers. We are ministering angels and that's who the sons of God are and that's what we do. We pray in the Spirit by praying in tongue and interceding for the problems of the world. We are intercessors and that's what God has given us the power to do.

We are sons of God, manifesting ourselves and making a different, we are making ourselves available by praying in the Spirit. We are building up our most Holy Faith by praying in the Holy Ghost. Yet we remain invisible to the church, because they fail to believe that they have the power to become sons of God. They rather continue to be called servants. The scripture said that we are no more servants but sons. God not only give the sons of God power to minister to the storms. He also gave us power to minister and set the captive free. Set free those who are in captivity. The Holy Spirit told me to pray to set the captive free that was about the later part of 2008. I didn't know who I was praying for. I thought maybe I was praying for the people in da-far since they were the only ones that I had heard about some bad things happening to them I didn't know anybody who were in captivity or in trouble. But I obeyed God and begin to pray for the captive to be set free as God commanded me to do. I would pray in tongue and pray in an understanding, because I didn't know who I was praying for. Praying in tongue is praying in the Holy Spirit. Only God know what you are saying unless he wanted it to be interpreted. That was the first time God ever told me to pray for those who are in captivity, though I didn't know anybody was in captivity but I was obedient to the Holy Spirit. I was praying for every nation the Holy Spirit had me travailing and tossing and turning sometimes all night long. I was crying and sometimes in pain. My stomach was in knots. I was in so much agony yet I continue to pray over and over Lord set the captive free and bring the perpetrator to justice. I didn't know what was going on. In about three weeks the story came out on the news about the woman in Australia, by the name of Elisabeth Fritzl who was held in captivity and kept in a cellar underground for twenty four years by her father, Josef Fritzl. She had not seen the light of day for 24 years. While in there he fathered seven children with his own daughter. Though he doesn't know it, but God made him let her go and he is in prison right now for life, I'm sure many of you know the story. I had no idea who I was praying for but God knew and told me to pray to set the captive free and God had mercy on her. We need more sons of God to pray and intercede for the nations. There is so much suffering in the world. There are more being held captive I don't know who they are. I don't know if they have been set free by now or not, that was in 2008 when Holy Spirit said there are two in the Los Angeles area who are being held captive. A few years ago there was a war that broke out that God wanted stopped immediately. He used me to say the words that I want this war to stop right now. After hearing the media on CNN say that it's going to be months before this war ends, as soon as he said that, the Holy Spirit spoke these words through my mouth, and said "Lord I want this war to end now and I mean right now" and it ended that night. That was Gods doing. I am trying to let you know that with God all things are possible. I am just a vessel that God used; he just used me to say the words that he wanted said.

Today my sister Alma was reminiscing on how God saved her sons life and how God used me to pray with her to save him. He was in prison and he called his mom and told her that some of the inmates were plotting to kill him that night. Alma got on the phone and called for the Head Officials that was in authority, so she could ask him to please move her son to a safe place. But the person in authority had left for the evening. She pleaded for the Night Official to move him and to please save her son's life. She said please move him to a safe place, but to no avail. She continued to call, all she got from him was I'm sorry I don't have that authority therefore I can't move him. My sister Alma called me and by faith we prayed that God would intercede and touch the heart of the Prison Official and cause him to save her sons life. She called back to talk with him and this time he said ok I'm going to do it, I might lose my job but I'm going to do it. I will keep him with me tonight. Thank God for touching his heart, later he told Alma that he had said to himself that her son was probably a gang member who just wanted to be with his gang members, but that was not the case he was not a gang member. God touched the Prison Official's heart and answered our prayers and saved her son's life. If you have faith the size of a mustard seed you can speak to the mountain and it shall be moved: And nothing shall be impossible unto you. (Matt.17:20). Faith is the most powerful thing there is, some people say prayer is the most powerful thing there is, but no its not, when you pray without faith you pray amiss. Prayer with faith will move mountains. The effectual fervent prayers of a righteous man availeth much: (James 5:16), (righteous means faith). It doesn't take a lot of people praying to move God. All it take is somebody who have faith and a sincere heart, when a person want to call everybody that they know to pray for them, it's for the lack of understanding or it's a sign that they don't have faith. It's better that you only tell one person or maybe two, who you believe can get a prayer though to God, who will stand in agreement with you and petition God on your behave and thank him for the victory. We know that all of his promises are yea, yea and amen. God said where two or three come together touching and agreeing on anything it shall be done. The bad thing about calling a lot of people to pray for you, some people never stop talking and saying negative things and you don't need that. They don't need to be praying for anybody except themselves that they might get delivered.

Jesus said all power is in his hand and he released his power to us the believers. Therefore we have his power to use according to his will. God have used me to intercede again for a young woman who he wanted to set free from the bondage of captivity. The Holy Spirit spoke to me and said "start praying again to set the captive free" That was August 15th 2009 and August 27th 2009 Jaycee Dugard was set free from her captor. She was kidnapped at eleven years old, and was kept in captivity for eighteen years until God set her free. And again, to God be the glory. He is the one, if it had not been for God I wouldn't have ever known to pray for anybody in captivity. I thank God that he loved and cared so much for those two women; Jaycee Dugard and Elizabeth Fritzl, that he heard their cry and had mercy on them and had me to pray for their deliverance. And God delivered them, and once again he answered my prayers. You don't have to know somebody to pray for them. I always pray for every nation, which is also my calling. God gave me an intercessory prayer ministry, praying for people everywhere. I started writing this book in 2007. Today is May 11/2012. I went on the internet for the first time since Jaycee Dugard was set free from captivity. I wanted to read her story about how she survived and I am adding that to the rest of my story that I had already wrote in my book about her in August of 2009, I read where she said maybe there is a higher power, I want to say to Jaycee just in case you ever read this book, if there was not a higher power you would still be in captivity because God is the only one who knew where you were beside your captor. It was God who delivered you. He just told me to pray to set the captive free. I had no knowledge of anybody being in captivity. I'm sure your mom never stopped praying for you, but God have chosen vessels that he use to pray and intercede for his will to be done and that was the second time that God told me to pray to set the captive free, and each time somebody was miraculously set free within two to three weeks when I obeyed God and prayed. God saw your suffering and he loved you so much, please know there is a God who can be touched. It is devastating to even think about how many people might be in captivity and might not ever be set free and might be forgotten about and left to die by their captor and many are still being held captive. I want to encourage as many of you that will make yourselves available to God to pray these deliverance prayers. It is so much agony to even think about the suffering and the fears that these people go through, knowing that they might be totally forgotten about or something might happen to their captors and nobody else know where they are. Praying those kind of prayers are hard on the stomach. But is nothing compared to what they are going through. I thank God for counting me worthy to pray such prayers. I beseech you therefore, brethren, by the mercies of God, that ye present your bodies a living sacrifice, holy, acceptable unto God, which is your reasonable service. (Roman 12:1).

GOD TOLD ME TO
WRITE A BOOK

I heard God when he told me to write a book. I never dreamed that God would tell me to write a book so I said no, not me. I had never thought about writing a book and I sure didn't know that was God talking to me, until my mother call and confirmed it and said "God said for you to write a book. God always talked to my mom about her children, same as he does with me about my children, when God couldn't get through to us, he would talk to my mom. At that time I didn't know the voice of the Lord as I know it today. I have always tried to be obedient when I knew that God was saying something to me. Growing up we were taught in the church by the pastor that God would only talk to the Leader. If God said something to you many pastors would ask you why would God talk to you when he can talk to the pastor or why would God tell you something that he hasn't told the pastor and then he would say, God is not a God of confusion. I have learned that God will talk to whomsoever he wishes to talk to. You have to be willing to obey God's voice after he talk to you. After I **realized**

that was God who was talking to me I started trying to write a book. I wrote about 3 books that were never published. I was not financially able to publish them. But I was trying to do what God told me to do. Though I didn't feel that those was the books that he wanted me to write but in my spirit I know this is the book that he wanted me to write. Those books were not bad. I still might one day be blessed to publish them. The titles were Revelation Knowledge of Jesus Christ, Troubled and Broken Marriages and Evangelism, maybe it was not time for this book at that time, I believe now is the time. I know now is the time to let God be true and live.

I owe my boldness to write this book to God and the Lakeland revivalist, Todd Bentley. I have never seen such boldness and energy and anointing in another human being. I was watching television as he was teaching on why some may or may not get their healing and it looked as though he had given all that he knew to give and wanted to give more. He was so over whelmed and so anointed and hungry for more and that's when God told me to e-mail him and tell him to tell the people to repent and live and the healing would come on them more abundantly. Instead of saying come up and accept the Lord Jesus so when you die you will go to heaven, just say accept the Lord Jesus and live. That's what Jesus said; repent you and live. My question is why heal a person if all they expect to do is keep on preparing to die. It's good sense to say accept the Lord and live since you are trying to get healed. When you say accepts the Lord, just end it by saying and live: just take a chance and try it and see what will begin to happen, Jesus said repent ye and live, his words are so powerful.

Who has satisfied thy mouth with good things so that thy youth is renewed like the eagle's (Psalms 103:5). This scripture is not talking about what you eat it's talking about what you say. Spoken words are powerful. Life and death is in the power of the tongue so be careful what you say. Jesus told his disciples to go and preach the gospel to every nation, heal the sick, raise the dead and cast out devils and preach the kingdom of God. He didn't say preach heaven. They prayed that his kingdom would come and you don't have to die to enter into the kingdom. God don't want you to die, God want you to live. Just tell the people to come up and receive the Lord Jesus as your personal savior that you might live. What do you have to lose? Jesus said if a man, keep my saying he will never die. (John 8:51). Many people don't accept what this scripture say because they don't believe it, or they have not heard it preached. It took a lot of boldness and energy for me to write a book as this. I thank God for the boldness. I received healing of arthritis in my knee from that healing revival. I have been healed so many times. I was miraculously healed in 1985 of stomach cancer.

I was inspirited by the Lakeland Revivalist and given the courage to do what God told me to do and that was to write this book. It takes lot of courage to write a book like this. This book could cause much controversy by those who don't believe the gospel of Jesus Christ. Thank God for putting me in touch with a spirit filled and knowledgeable teacher on eternal life, Dr. Harlo White ministry has had such an impact on my life, with his Kingdom teaching on Eternal Life and the cell structures and so much more… I pray God by his grace and mercy that he will bless everyone who read this book; and open the eyes of their understanding that they might know you and know what the hope of your calling is. I ask this in Jesus name, Amen.

Author: Zelma High Money